JOHN MC

THE BEST
(including quite the worst)
OF DIDYMUS

ILLUSTRATIONS BY AUTHOR

First published in *Resurgence* Magazine,
Ford House, Hartland, Bideford, Devon EX39 6EE
www.resurgence.org

This edition is published by Resurgence Books

© John Moat

The right of John Moat to be identified as author of this work
has been asserted by him in accordance with
the Copyright, Designs and Patents Act 1988

ISBN 978 1 900322 22 5

Designed and set by Simon Willby
With thanks to Juliette Collins and Lorna Howarth

Printed by Imprint Digital

FOREWORD
HUMOUR REPRIEVE

ONE OF THE many perks of being in the *Resurgence* editorial team is the opportunity to read great pearls of wisdom that are cast upon our desks each day, in the form of articles and reviews. Some are rather weighty and philosophical, some are full of good ideas and solutions, but none is more seized-upon than the 'Didymus' column, written by long-time contributor and dear friend, John Moat.

Seeing the endearingly low-tech, typewritten pages and accompanying zany illustration, signals that it is time once again to make a pot of coffee, to sit in the office 'comfy chair' and relax in the knowledge that a humour-reprieve is imminent. The ensuing titters, nay, gales of laughter serve only to draw others to the page, as the article gets passed around the office and fills us all with the light relief that is Didymus.

Yet tucked-away in each piece is that gem - the wondrously good idea - that shines its light through the fug of hilarity; that filters back in conversation or on a subsequent read as a real solution to many a crisis of our time; as a counter-balance to the problems posed by those media-types who choose only to focus on despair. When, for example, will The Great Tax Reform be given the credit it deserves?

I'd vote for John Moat as our local MP any time, but I'm sure he wouldn't be the least-bit seduced! So his voice will remain that of poet, storyteller, cricketing commentator and our much-beloved Didymus The Profound.

Lorna Howarth, Co-editor, Resurgence magazine

DEDICATION

DON'T REALLY see any option but to dedicate this book to John Fairfax, one time Poetry Editor of *Resurgence* and inventor of the Murphy's Inflatable Pleasure Dome which was first featured in the Didymus column thus, alas, ensuring that it was denied essential government Research & Development funding so that it remains un-deployed in the world's trouble spots where it could be achieving international accord and détente…at least until the morning after.

ALSO BY JOHN MOAT

POETRY
Thunder of Grass
6d per annum
Skeleton Key
Fiesta & Fox Reviews His Prophesy
The Welcombe Overtures
Firewater & the Miraculous Mandarin
Practice (with drawings)
The Valley (with drawings)
100 Poems
Hermes & Magdalen

NOVELS
Heorot
Bartonwood
Mai's Wedding
The Missing Moon

SHORT STORY
Rain

ALSO
The Founding of Arvon
The Standard of Verse

And with John Fairfax
The Way to Write

CONTENTS

8	A MORATORIUM ON MIRTH
12	THE ALTERNATIVE COLD
16	REGILLATIONS
20	A TOUCH OF THE EAST
24	BACKACHE
28	IF YOU CAN'T LICK'EM
32	SCHELL SHOCK
36	NOUVELLE VAGUE
40	GOOD SCHOOLING
44	WAITING FOR THE CALL
48	FLANNELLING
52	SHARING THE JOKE
56	AFTER THOUGHT
60	VAGUELY GREEN
64	The Great Tax REFORM!
72	THE RESURGENCE BARK or ATTENTION ALL SHIPPING (Written for Resurgence 25th anniversary)
78	EXPERTS
82	SPORTING GREEN
86	JUST A FEW QUESTIONS
90	PROGRESS - A BACKWARD GLANCE
94	ANOTHER FINE LETTUCE
98	NEXT TIME ROUND
102	SWALLOWED
106	SCREEN TEST
110	AS FAR AS IT GOES
114	PADDED UP
118	AND LEAVE THE HOUSE FREE
123	TWENTY-TWENTY VISION
127	THE GREEN PLANET
131	GREEN SMOKE
135	GOVERNESS
139	TIME FOR A YARN

A MORATORIUM ON MIRTH

THEN THIS MORNING we hear of Sakharov's arrest.

The other night, on my way home from the pub, I was taken by storm. I was thinking how the deadly game of liar dice being waged by the largely self-appointed leaders of the world has brought not just humankind but the gem of Earth as never before to the brink. While we, that is virtually the entire world, like the helpless dependants of a crazy gambler, have to sit by and watch the brinkmanship get out of control. In numb disbelief we listen to the bidding. They've already lost their shirts, so when it comes to the last throw what's left for a stake? House? Land? But that's never enough, not on the last throw. What's left? The gamblers look round. The wild gaze falls on us.

I drove up the bank. With leaders like these, who needs enemies? And then there is another question, so simple that finding words to frame it is agony. Who, and I mean who, who do these leaders represent? The people of the world? The people of the world just want to be left in peace.

Back on the road, I began work on the Declaration.

Now, I should make it clear that this wasn't conceived as a private gesture. This was to be the beginning of something big. *Resurgence*, that would be the initial vehicle, the agent of contagion. From it's inside cover the word would spread around the world like Asian Flu in a muggy winter. My initial draft might not be the whole ticket, but the canvassed power of the Alternative Mind would soon have it in shape. Then just sit back and watch.

A matter of weeks and every Kremlin and Pentagon would be grinding to a halt under the weight of paper. The in-trays, the corridors, the forecourts — sack upon sack of declaration slips, each signed by a genuine, *bona fide* representative of humankind. And then in every democratic country, on voting day, what a turnout, and what a crush of paper in the ballot-boxes! But where are the voting-slips? There aren't very many, and those are difficult to find among the bulk of signed declarations. The results are declared. The swing away from the government is in favour of humankind.

Here is the Declaration. You will appreciate that I had to finish it before I got home, so it is just a first draft.

I, the undersigned, hereby serve notice that I no longer accept the authority of any government or system of power that disobeys the survival wishes of humankind.

The government, therefore, can count on my support only if it is prepared to do these two things:

1. Establish by referendum what proportion of the inhabitants of this country would have the leaders of every country in the world renounce force (by nuclear or conventional means) as a way of resolving the differences between people and nations.

2. Campaign by every possible peaceful means to ensure that the governments of all other nations do the same.

I believe that at this crucial time any government unprepared to do this or, in the event of a referendum in favour of the renunciation of force, unprepared to cooperate with other nations to implement disarmament, cannot be said to represent the will of its people, and is wholly discredited.

That should do the trick.

Sakharov arrested. It is despair, hopelessness, above all the shrugged shoulder, that frightens me. The feeling that there is nothing left worth a try. There's a lot of this hopelessness around at the moment, often under the sham guise of heroic realism. Here is Professor George Steiner quoted in *The Listener*:

"As I meet them now, the young name no place where they want to be, or which excites them, or to which they're travelling the next summer in order to help build. The great dream of the Kibbutz, in the larger sense...seems to have been flogged out of us...

"Why did we let ourselves be seduced by the great dream? They were, I think, enormously creative mistakes, enormously creative fantasies. What really scares me at the moment is: how do we operate without such windows? What happens when there is the insight or the conviction or the instinct that, whatever you do, you'll get it wrong?"

Well! Was ever the challenge to Alternative Movement more clearly stated? To our intellectuals if you want it, but in chief to every one of us who ventures in the field. The imperative is so clear. Whatever we do we must continue with it until we see that it works. Because at this time anything that works, and continues to work, provides all of us a window, yes, and perhaps also a door.

I seem to be getting serious. God forbid…

At this point I remembered something that William Yeats wrote and went to find it. On the way I came across this, "Civilization too, will that not also destroy where it has loved, until it shall bring the simple and the natural things again, and a new Argo with all the gilding of her bows sail out to find another Fleece."

But that wasn't what I was after. I wanted something on the danger of a world that collapsed into seriousness, "… for only when we are gay over a thing, and can play with it, do we show ourselves its master, and have minds clear enough for strength." Amen.

I wonder if you remember the legend of a tumbler who unrolled his carpet in the way of the marching army. Sakharov if it could summon a smile that would strengthen your mind and noble heart I would fall on my face.

Issue 79 - March/April 1980

THE ALTERNATIVE COLD

WITH THE EVENING drawing in and a new season of rheums upon us, it is arguably – arguably, you've probably come across this handy new piece of jargon: it means, what I'm about to say is entirely without foundation but I'll be blowed if I don't say it just the same – an appropriate time for me to publish the findings of a quarter of a century's research, often extremely hazardous, into alternative medicine.

I came to the business at eighteen by way of a cold. Yet another cold. The person sitting next to me on the bus said I should take a cup of tea made with a clove of garlic, and that would do the trick. He was a pale, thin man who based his authority on the impression he'd probably drop dead if anyone so much as sneezed. I did what he said. But being green to the *materia medica* I got the prescription wrong and made the tea from a bulb of garlic and a sprinkling of cloves. That was one hell of a cup of tea. I don't remember what happened to the cold, but it was a week before anyone again sat next to me on the bus.

For my next cold I was staying with my mother. My mother was 'done for' daily by an oak-hearted cockney lady who did for her the same as she'd done for no less than Sir Winston Churchill in his bunker during the war. She said that the only cure for a cold (and one habit she'd acquired from Sir Winston was not being argued with) was something called 'egg-op'. She told me how to make it. Ginger, a pint of stout and a raw egg, well mulled. It sounded tasty, I gave it a try. I think maybe she got the 'mulled' in the wrong place. The stuff was chunky, it looked like a cross between a khaki scrambled egg and a yoghurt culture with a heavy nose-cold. I needed a spoon to get it down. What was required to keep it down I never did discover. I think there may be more to that title of Winston Churchill's, 'The Darkest Hour', than historians have hitherto understood. I think I know why he stuck to the brandy.

And speaking of brandy puts me in mind of my latest cure. This winter, thanks to regular gargling with pure lemon-juice, daily superdoses of rosehip and ascorbic acid, and each night remembering to switch on the ioniser, I nearly survived without a cold. But no, the end of March it got me. I hit it with everything. *Arsenicum* at the first sniff; then because of the muggy weather and the sore throat, *gelsemium*; then when the wind shifted cold and dry to the East, *aconite*; and finally, when it threatened my chest, *bryonia*. I tried to starve it out, and to overwhelm it with toddies and blistering grogs. Not a blind bit of use. And it didn't get better.

In desperation I called at the local health-store, went browsing along the shelves, hoping the old wives had come up with something new. Suddenly I stopped 'on point' – the small brown bottle. The goose-pimples started on my neck, I might have been recognising something from a previous incarnation. *Fine Old Indian Brandee.* On the label a picture of a chieftain in his war-feathers. There were two bottles left. I snapped them up. It was big medicine – tasted of wig-wam and the changing-room after a lively sundance. And the instructions implied one should have plenty. What's more it worked. Within a week my cold had begun to waver. I can't recommend it too strongly. It's manufactured by: British Chemotheutic Products Ltd, Bradford.

Incidentally, a day or two after my recovery I heard a boffin on the radio announcing his findings. His statistics showed that the people who get the most colds tend to be the nervy, neurotic sort, the ones who think they're going to get a cold. That's interesting. I'll look into that next winter.

My attention has not however been confined to the common cold. One of my most spectacular and perilous research projects was into little known cures for fibrositis. For years, on the recommendation of a Hartland man, I'd been treating all aches with something, called Stone's Devonshire Oil. The label said it cured everything from mastitis to black udder and it was hot stuff. You needed to be in the pink of condition to survive that cure. But then one day I was having my neck put back by an osteopath. He diagnosed fibrositis around the shoulders and said the best cure he knew was an application of stinging nettles. Something to do with uric acid. I wasn't tempted – not that is until some time later at a conference. I had a pain in my shoulder, had come without my Devonshire Oil, was looking out of my bedroom window, and there were these nettles. I slunk out a back way and went and grasped a bunch. Back in my room, stripped to the waist, teeth clenched, I was lashing myself about the shoulders when a friend knocked to call me to a meeting. I thought I'd show him my mettle, and called him in. It wasn't my friend. It was a girl come to make the bed. She said she was sorry for disturbing me, and that she could just as easily do the bed later.

For kidney and bladder complaints there were de Witt's pills. They had an impressive potency that made one's pee blue – bright, startling electric blue. I bought them for my friends, and administered them for every complaint from sunburn to insomnia, just to see the look on their faces next morning when they came out of the lavatory. One strapping, bull-chested friend presented me with a problem: he'd never had a thing wrong with him in his life. But I had the inspiration to tell him the pills were what were sold in our parish as the world's most explosive aphrodisiac. He took a couple, and a third for good measure. Next morning was a let down. He mentioned he'd peed blue as one might mention the weather, and then got on with his breakfast. But I did hear from him a month later. He wrote that he had become engaged. The p.s. read, "and you were absolutely right about those pills."

I do, though, know of one cure that is priceless and simple and about as alternative as you can get. And what's more it is for one of the most painful of all minor ailments, namely the sty. At the first prick of a sty, run for a potato. Grate it, and make a poultice of it. Keep it on the eye for at least half an hour, or if the timing is right, sleep with it on. I acknowledge that *pulsatilla* is good for stys. But the potato – it obliterates them. I've never known it to fail.

If in the next twenty-five years I come upon any other foolproof cure, I'll let you know.

Issue 82 - September/October 1980

REGILLATIONS

THE ANNUAL AGRICULTURAL and Horticultural Census form has arrived. It may be easy for some, but we have 2. 4047 hectares of land, and the Ministry has given me less than a week to fill it in. They do however, bless their hearts, give us Notes for Guidance...twenty-one of them. This one is No. 18: *Seasonal or Casual workers are workers, family and hired, who are not regular workers but are working on the holding on 1 June including those supplied temporarily by agricultural contractors or gang-masters.* Gang-masters, blimey! No, I'll never have this form completed in a week.

All this care and attention isn't as recent as I'd imagined. I've been reading Sidney J. Jury's collection of Devonshire Chatter, and have discovered that the authorities were properly concerned as far back as 1926. Here are a couple of extracts from Jan Stewer's *Rules and Regillations for the hindrance of all Varmers and sitch as keeps cows:*

16

INSPECTORS. All Cowsheds must be ready for inspection at any time o' day or night by eether o' the following people: ... Local Sanitary Authority, Skule Attendance Ossifer, Council Surveyor, Medical Ossifer of Health, Boy Scouts, Girls Guides, Cap'm of Vire Brigade, the Mimber of Parlyment and the Distric' Nurse. If eether-one of these people pays a visit to the varm the Varmer must leave whatever 'e's about and go 'round and assist 'em to poke their noses into his business. If he don't he'll be vined vive pound.

REGILLATIONS FOR VARMERS. All Varmers mus' zee that their cows eyes is properly attended to, and if they'm short-zighted they mus' be pervided with sparticles. Otherwise they'm ap' to overlook the mangle and go short, and the varmer will be vined vive pound...

If the cow flinks his tail in the milker's eye or putts his voot in the bucket, the milker is allowed to say, "Bother it" or "Dear, dear". If he says, "Darn your stubid eyes, I'll skin you alive if you daun' bide still" he'll be vined vive pound. . And if 'tis zummin wiss than that he'll be vined more, up to tain pound, according to the wissness.

NOTICE. The above regillations is just to go on with. If it should be found that any Varmers and Cowkeepers is still making a living the ole Parleyment will think out some more.

I suppose this was a joke. I suppose too it was a joke when it was announced on the radio that the latest Common Market Regulation was applicable to the wearing of shoes in wet weather. In wet weather all pedestrians are obliged to wear shoes with standard regulation Common Market non-slip soles, and when precipitation is forecast they must not leave the house without having such shoes about their person. Policemen and traffic war-dens to be empowered to make spot-checks. Well, I didn't know it was a joke. Even when someone told me it was April 1st I wasn't convinced. Come to think of it, I'm still not convinced.

In an article in *The Listener* Robert Hughes describes the architecture of New York State's seat of government, Albany Mall. "It is designed for one purpose and achieves it perfectly: it expresses the centralisation of power, and one may doubt if a single citizen has ever wandered on its bleak plaza, so out of scale that even the marble facing seems like white Formica, and felt the slightest connection with the bureaucratic and governmental processes going on in the towers above him. Its meaning is utterly simple; there are no ambiguities. All the joys of minimalism are there. What speaks from those stones is not the difference between American free enterprise and, say, Russian socialism, but the similarities between the corporate and bureaucratic states of mind, irrespective of country or ideology. One could see any building at Albany Mall with an eagle on top, or a swastika, or a hammer and sickle; it makes no difference to the building."

Two or three years ago there was a story in our local paper. Joe Mikita had been blind seventeen years, the result of a gelignite explosion. Recently he'd been sent on a £1,000 training course and thereby had secured a job at The Royal Bristol Workshops. This required him to move from his home in Devon. The job was to be financed with a grant from the Devon County Council. Forty-eight hours before departure, all packed and ready to go, he received a letter from the County Council...by second class mail...telling him the grant had been cancelled. Mekita was quoted as saying, "The news came as a stab in the back. It was so unexpected after everything was in the bag. As far as engineering is concerned I can work side by side with any capstan operator. But the future holds nothing for me now...this job was my big hope." Mr Hanson, the county council's social services director, said the late notification to Mr Mekita was "slightly regrettable" - the appointment had been approved, he said, on the assumption that the present level of expenditure would continue, but this had not been the case.

It's not that bureaucracies recruit among the inhuman. It has to be that inhuman structures and systems produce, as Schumacher so often pointed out, a behaviour to which individual humanity is neither relevant nor plausible.

The hand that signed the paper felled a city;
Five sovereign fingers taxed the breath,
Doubled the globe of dead and halved a country;
These five fingers did a king to death.

It doesn't matter whether the issue is Joe Mikita, or Windscale, or Auschwitz, the hand that signs the paper is never answerable... least of all to that painful individual heart-tissue that would make it uncomfortable to live with the consequences of its signature.

A hand rules pity as a hand rules heaven;
Hands have no tears to flow.

Dylan Thomas, it seems, understood how in a successful bureaucracy the decision is not actually made by any *one*.

I remember now, I was going to write an irate rate-payer's letter about Joe Mikita's treatment. But you know how it is, the days go by... It occurs to me that Pontius Pilate is the patron not only of bureaucrats. The decision is somebody else's. One is busy. Finally one washes one's hands.

Issue 88 - September/October 1981

A TOUCH OF THE EAST

I TOO WAS BORN in India. The youngest son of the Raj, I came to Earth in impeccable circumstances in a British nursing-home in Mussoorie. This event less than a month after and not more than a hundred miles or so away from that nativity in the desert of Rajasthan which featured our Editor, no doubt as a pie-faced example of *Resurgence*-accredited natural delivery. Alas, how it is vain to question one's karma! But even if I was deported after a mere six weeks, no matter - I'd chalked up my credentials. A child of the Orient, it is noticeable that I have virtually no problem with my ego. Logic, that Western foible, I am untouched by it. As a cricketer I possess, I've always considered, an unpredictable natural flare. And that of

course is how you get to write under the cover of *Resurgence*.

My authority thus established, I had been about to make hot curry of the current vogue for honouring all things Eastern to the detriment and denial of Western culture and its achievements, when my Raj blood was distracted by a crowning nostalgia - the sound of the gunboats putting to sea. All of a sudden it is the Falkland Island issue.

Last week I heard on the radio Alastair Cook's *Letter from America*. He was talking about the Falkland crisis, and incidentally regretting the technology that makes it possible for a correspondent's despatch to be pre-recorded. In the early days, when he had to address his audience live, then it was possible to be up to the minute. Whereas now, with instant global communication, if a recording is shelved for a matter of hours, it is liable to be "overtaken by events". He should complain! Publication of this live despatch is two months away. The British have just retaken South Georgia, our Iron Lady is demonstrating what can be achieved in less than no time with a chest-expander, and God only knows what's coming up fast in the outside lane.

Some twenty years ago I had a dream which, I remember, clung to me for days. Eventually it came away in a poem. Here's a bit of it:

She was stopping to dispute his stare,
But I saw in the figure only a remnant of war
Who tottered on bone-stumps, his feet being all blown
To hell. He smiled. His smile was in his skull. "Take care,"
I whispered. "He's dead, but his finger remembers to fight.
He'll still mow you down...Then stay, but I shall go on."
And so awoke...

I still find that statement curious. The old War-Game, it won't lie down. I believe (some days merely half-believe) that consciousness, through the Gethsemane (Kipling's connotation) of the Somme, and out of the crucifixion of the holocaust, did achieve the shift. But as yet it has not unscrambled the blood-code. The blood remains programmed. Each seven years in its bath the blind monster stirs - and, bleep, bleep, his puppet-despots respond. They press the button and his high-protein diet, the young and proud, are fed in on the old conveyor. I think one can still sense those dread fateful moments when the Valkyries, who run riot before the carnage, come galloping across the sky. The earth shivers. So what's ever to disarm them? Consciousness? Consciousness could - if there were enough of it around, and if it could somehow get between the joints of the trigger finger. I don't know what way there is of promoting consciousness, except perhaps by the individual effort at any cost to stay in touch with it. And to help do that perhaps it makes sense to pray.

Tick tock, the Ship of Fools sets sail. Is there nothing good that can come of it? Thomas Blackburn, in his poem, *Before Gaza*, wrote:

When Cain strikes Abel to the ground,
You must not reason why,
Some dream clears with those battering fists
A blemished blood-shot eye.

I think I believe that too. Though the scenario does alter a jot if Brother Cain has built himself a nuclear arsenal and Abel an independent deterrent. Damn and blast these armaments! One thing this Falkland Islands show seems to demonstrate is that where weapons, say a costly fleet, exist their employment becomes for the politician not so much a matter of choice as a matter of existential necessity. Which puts me in mind of one thing I hope won't have happened between now and the time this *Resurgence* reaches you. I hope that the huge focus of concern for peace and disarmament planned to coincide with the U.N. Special Session on Disarmament in June is not distracted or upstaged by...no, you'll have to excuse me, at present I'm not looking for words to describe it.

General Eisenhower was a funny old soldier. I read this week that when he was President he said, "Every gun that is made, every warship launched, every rocket fired, signifies, in a final sense, a theft from those who hunger and are not fed, from those who are cold and are not clothed."

Finally I'd better let you in on my keenest, my real motivating anxiety. I tell you, if these Argentinians get us slung out of the World Cup, if throughout long hot June I have to sit, without partisan interest, listening to some other country's beer-cans rattling onto the pitch... The thought of it! Just as well I was born in India and inherited these marvellous powers of non-attachment, this clear-eyed serenity, this... Ah, that's what I'll do, I'll emigrate. Except it can't be India. As far as I know the Indians don't even have a football team. I don't suppose they even have a football.

Issue 93 - July/August 1982

BACKACHE

Now for my review of New Age orthopaedic techniques with special and arresting reference to problems of the back - my back.

Precocious in malfunction, my first seizure happened as the result of an accident in the school rifle-range. I was having a trial for the cadet-force shooting team when the R.S.M. blew up behind his binoculars. He'd spotted that I'd placed five shots in and around the bull on my neighbour's target. The R.S.M.'s expletive carried the clout of a sidewinder missile. My back locked, and I was a stretcher case. In those days osteopathy was very much on the fringe. My mother's interest, however, was beyond the fringe - a healer in Portsmouth with fingers like wire-cutters and a hold over the fringe housewives of Hampshire that would have impressed Rasputin. He unpicked me in no time. But the flaw had been established. I never did make the shooting team. To this day I remain target-shy.

At University my back became increasingly liable. Once it locked at 2 a.m. when I was climbing into college, half through a small first floor window. It was a close-run thing whether I was done inside by the sub-rector, or outside by the police.

Often life's most formative events result from a seemingly insignificant accident. So it was with my introduction to chiropractic. I was in London, Stanhope Gardens, parking my minibus in a narrow space. I was in gear, reverse, half-standing on the pedals to see out of the back window when - crick. I was locked. I couldn't take my foot off the clutch for fear of ramming the Austin Princess behind, and I couldn't reach the ignition. I couldn't move. I started to yell to pedestrians, but their response was to run for it. Until at last an Indian (may his line increase!), probably nerved for this sort of spectacle by the performance of fakirs, stopped to chat. He'd not been in the country long, so language was a problem. After a time I think he deduced I was in some form of ecstatic trance and began to tip-toe away. But by redoubling my shrieks I managed to persuade him back and, at last, to turn off the engine. At this point another passer by stopped and he told me that there was, right across the street, this chiropractor.

An Australian of tart demeanour and awesome strength he'd discovered his gift as a kind of tangent to the back-breaking business of working in the mines somewhere near Broken Hill. That experience had equipped him with the graphic vocabulary he used to depict the benefits of his favoured side-line - and this he saw as the true panacea - colonic irrigation. When he'd unclicked me and clicked me back together again as if I was a slightly-worn leggo set, he said I could do with a colonic irrigation. This, I confess, sounded to me beyond the fringe. I got out by promising to retail his good news to my mother.

My back continued to deteriorate and to cause embarrassment and public alarm. Once Antoinette, that's my wife, and I were walking out of the British Consulate in Florence, when I got the grab. With a scream I went down, locked, on the floor, and the ceremonial *carabiniere* who was guarding the place had his sword out in a flash. When he could detect no assailant he came over and prodded me with his sword, gingerly, as if I might be a letter-bomb. Antoinette after research discovered that in Italy there is no fringe, only the beyond, and so carted me off into the Tuscan hills in search of this *contadino* who had, it was said, a knack. He operated on the kitchen table, was reassuringly unpainless and excellent except that repeated demonstrations of his knack, encouraged by repeated injections of lira, never got me further than the bottom of his front steps. Later, back and immovable in our *pensione*, I remembered I'd once (and I can't unless our Editor were to grant me the entire issue explain how) been the guest of a remarkable spiritualist, teacher and dowser who lived in Fiesole, just outside Florence. We gave him a ring. He said he'd have a word with his guide, who was a Red Indian chief called, I seem to remember, Red Bull. Later he rang back and told me not to worry, Red Bull had the matter in hand. Our *pensione* that night felt a little eerie, I mean it's one thing to be manipulated by an Australian miner…It took me some time to get to sleep. But Red Bull (may his tribe increase!) did the trick. In the morning, tearful with gratitude and failing disbelief, I found myself perfectly in tact.

But not for long. My back continued to deteriorate. Finally I thought the fringe had been given a fair crack of the whip and consulted a conventional specialist. His methods may have been conventional, but certainly not he. Had he, as often appeared, been acting a character in the Brothers Karamazov one would still have judged him a shade excitable. Once, from his front door, seeing me overloading my spine by carrying my briefcase he threw a tantrum that stopped the traffic from Harley St to Marble Arch. For fifteen guineas he wrote me off, told me never to dig again and to come back in a month. He talked me into two tailor-made corsets, and ran something like a Black & Decker sander up and down my vertebrae. But my back continued to deteriorate.

It was then, some ten years ago, I came across the Alexander Technique. Ten years of sustained realisation that what one had finally understood "forward and up" to mean was nothing to do with what "forward and up" meant to Alexander. Perhaps I should leave someone else to explain. However I can record that within weeks of my first lesson I was out of pain. Now I'm digging again. My back is stronger than at any time since my accident in the rifle-range.

Issue 94 - September/October 1982

IF YOU CAN'T LICK'EM

SLUGS. I'M SORRY to bring up the subject, but I think we all realise that *Resurgence* is fast going to lead us nowhere in this New Age if it's not prepared to chew on the unpalatable, the deep-rooted problems. The problems that won't go away. Like slugs. Or, to be more specific, like the problem I'm having with the slugs in my garden.

You probably remember Witherington in the Ballad of Chevy Chase.

For Witherington needs must I wayle
As one in dolefull dumpes,
For when his leggs were smitten off,
He fought upon his stumpes.

This summer, in my vegetable patch, I've been thinking of Witherington. It's when I stand still for a minute and lean on my fork for a breather. I'm almost frightened to look down at my feet. Slugs. The little nifty ones in platoon strength; the brown, heavy-tracked jobs; and then the cruises, the great black slitherers…arrgh!

This morning I picked a Webbs Wonderful. It fell apart in a brown syrup. Twenty-seven! It's by counting, very carefully, one holds back the hysterics. If you can't eat your lettuce, at least you can be going for the record.

I'll tell you what I've tried so far. Grapefruit traps. Absurd, like putting out cheese for the mice in the hope they'll drop dead from insomnia. Beer traps. Absurd, if there's one thing worse than a slug, it's twenty-thousand slugs with a bad hangover. Ducks. Maybe I got the wrong ducks. Our ducks were interested only in waddling into my study and having a simulated splash-in on the white round duck-pond shaped deep-piled rug. We gave them to a more sensible neighbour. When the ducks didn't eat her slugs, she ate them. I've tried that white sprinkling stuff you can buy from Henry Doubleday's. Not a lot of use. Perhaps that's not fair, but I didn't detect its real worth until I'd given it up - slug density was suddenly so severe that understandably they had to appropriate the greenhouse. I've tried all the killers money can buy in the local garden shops. And if that admission leaves a scorch mark on the cover of *Resurgence* then I may as well come clean and add that, given my present mood, should a man wearing a Porton Down Cricket Club tie happen at my door selling bin-ends in unlabelled rusty canisters, and say they spell Doomsday for the slimy gastropod, then, if I couldn't get to Ford House in about ten minutes for ideological re-education, I just might be extremely interested.

You blanch. Well let me tell you, unconfirmed reports have been reaching me that Lawrence D. Hills himself is being given a rough ride by the dread *limacidæ*. At the same time reliable but undisclosed sources close to the Dail suggest that John Seymour, faced with the threat of the Irish slug, has suspended the talks on the minimum deterrent. That old theory about good compost producing a fit lettuce with vibes strong enough to break a slug's tooth, I suspect it's going to have to be rewritten.

I'm not tearing into this subject without having given it a deal of thought. One thought I've had is this. Maybe by the very nature of things there had to be the flaw, the germ of what went wrong. Maybe there is nothing in the universe that does not carry the trademark and signature of the Great Creator. Except the slug. Maybe the slug is the one that slipped through the wire. When did you ever hear anyone who had a good word to say for a slug? Maybe on His *tabla rasa*, on Her unbounded drawing-board there was suddenly this inexplicable inkblot (I mean it happens to us all), and the Almighty said, "Yee-uk! The only word to describe you is: Slug. Go on, get lost." And then just sat there and watched as the black blot slithered away, a trail of slime straight into the proto-patch of Webbs Wonderfuls.

I confessed this thought the other day to a *Resurgence* reader. She looked severe and said that mine was the sort of attitude which if noticed might lead to a real formative shock next time round, my next moment of re-entry. I'd probably come back as a slug or something. That shook me. But then I began to think about that too. Since on current form I'm not in any case likely to make a golf-professional by my next time round; since it's the destiny of just about every slug in the universe to be bedded out in my garden; since at last I've got the soil in pretty good heart and, besides, can't think of anywhere I'd rather be; since if I were being a full-time slug I'd at least not be being old wellie-boots breaking into the patch with the metaldehyde; and since I was in any event about due for the lift of consciousness that'll fetch me up on some dreary, redemptive, vegan diet…to hell with it! Vive la limace! I just could be on to a winning ticket.

Issue 95 - November/December 1982

SCHELL SHOCK

THE 1.25 TO PADDINGTON, settling down to coffee, a couple of golf biscuits and a good beguiling book. *The Fate of the Earth* by Jonathan Schell. By the time we rattle through Tiverton Junction I'm onto the hard stuff and watching out of the corner of my eye the fellow across the corridor with the plug in his ear. If I see him duck I'll know it's the three minute warning.

Schell-shock, a bad attack, and I'm caught without my *arnica*.

Schell's achievement is that he has constructed a lens which enables the reader, before he quite knows what's happening, to have stared into the melting heart of the fireball without going totally blind. Usually if we try to contemplate extinction, not just personal extinction but the extinction of all recognisable life, we treat ourselves to an experience similar to (though I confess the scars of my authority are merely hearsay) being eaten alive by a tiger. Some inner anaesthetic is released. This means that even when the big chap gets as far as our elbow, we're still able to say: "Euk, what a mess! Damn glad that sort of thing could never happen to me."

But Schell not only holds us there riveted, awake to a sickening imminence, but the whole operation is managed without even a local anaesthetic. The result is extraordinary. We feel still very much on the danger list, but somehow revived. The secret is, I think, that by the scope of his courage, and the excellence and simplicity of his writing, he makes the holocaust imaginable. Now that is important. When something is unimaginable it is beyond our control. And if it is a threat that is unimaginable, then that threat assumes a demonic wayward power. But render it imaginable and it is somewhat defused; it is brought within the compass of conscious acceptance - or rejection.

I have this friend who is upper brass in the Country Civil Service. He's a bunker man. This means that in the event of a you-know-what he is *ex officio* entitled to special luncheon vouchers and the key to the bunker. He was telling me last week that every so often the lads go underground for a dress rehearsal. What he finds curious about these dummy-runs is that all simulated activity is on the assumption that nothing in the thermal pulse or the tricky firestorm has accidentally interfered with the existing telephone network. His wife then arrested the conversation by asking for bunker-guidance as to what she might most usefully do if the three-minute warning sounded when she was conducting playschool in the village hall. No messing - these civil servants are on top of their jobs. He suggested, straight off, that she and the children should get under the stage. Hee-hee-hee...excuse me! Anyway, that's what I mean by the danger of the unimaginable.

Schell's book is stupendous.

Whizzing through Westbury I had the fantasy of the House being kept in for disorderly conduct during P.M.'s question time and every man jack and jill of them being kept in while the Speaker reads from *The Fate of the Earth*. An idea almost as inspired as that one about the President being allowed to press the button only if he has first, with his bare hands, torn the heads off two or three dozen children.

The point that Schell's argument homes in on with the clout and single purpose of a heat-seeking missile is this: "If the argument about nuclear weapons is to be conducted in good faith, then just as those who favour the deterrence policy (not to speak of traditional military doctrine) must in all honesty admit that their scheme contemplates the extinction of humanity in the name of protecting national sovereignty, so must those who favour complete nuclear and conventional disarmament, as I do, admit that their recommendation is inconsistent with national sovereignty; to pretend otherwise would be to evade the political question central to the nuclear predicament." What he omits to say is that whatever national sovereignty may have once amounted to it is now defunct. The phrase has become either a byword for political face - or a euphemism for a nation's collective greed.

I more or less survive the journey to London, and am walking gingerly from Paddington Station when I read on a billboard that the Synod of the Church of England is "sitting on the Bomb". I snatch a cab and hurry to the Russian Embassy.

You don't believe me? Well it's true. The Pergamon Press is publishing the writings of Yuri Andropov and the Russian Ambassador is throwing a party to celebrate. There's been a slip of protocol and I've not personally been invited, but a friend of mine has, and we've agreed the embassy is where we should meet. The forecourt suggests that it's here they are holding the auditions for the re-make of The Spy who Came in From the Cold - all the minor parts, in particular the battalion of frontier police. Needless to say, it is snowing. I get caught up in the action, am escorted smartly into the entrance hall, am instructed to sit and wait, and have a press-release thrust into my hand which sheds reassuring light about the efforts for peace being indefatigably pursued by the Russian people. Reassuring because the glances and sub-zero demeanour of the numerous attendant officials might otherwise have me fooled. At last the guests are leaving. Nothing sub-zero about them: the vodka sings in their eyes and each is clutching his copy of General Secretary Andropov's new book. As my friend and I descend the icy steps two of the Equity hopefuls look up at us and smile sheepish as boys caught in the larder. On the bottom baluster they have just completed a perfect miniature snowman. He is plump, ten inches tall, seated and holding a staff. He's comfortable, a little Nikita Kruschev, and his face beams warm enough to melt the cold hearts of all the world.

The snowman's face has settled in my mind. It is company throughout the evening. And later, at dinner, when my friend regales me with quotations from the deliberating Synod, which he has overhead on the radio, including the Archbishop's "This is a moment to seek to stabilise the balance of terror," I think back to Jonathan Schell's book, and then I see the little snowman's beaming face. I smile, merely smile - but I feel I could almost die laughing. And it occurs to me that that might be the softest of all possible options.

Issue 98 - May/June 1983

NOUVELLE VAGUE

■ ■ ■ AND ANOTHER THING: is the Fourth World going to be any better a place for the frail dissenting minority. Is it going to protect our modest way of life from the reactionary heavy-hand of the patriarchy, the revisionist hoof of the motherhood, and the scorn of all those other beefy minorities (I haven't the courage to mention them by name) who through the formative years of pre-Aquarian persecution have built up so much social muscle and learned to carry such reformative clout?

I confess, I myself am only recently, as we minorities say, out of the closet. As a matter of fact it was in the closet that I first discovered my membership. I think, purely for the sake of clarity, I'll rephrase that. What I mean is that it was there I first discovered I was a member of this minority. I was reading a back-number of *The Listener*, and came across an extract from an interview with our champion Benedict Nightingale. Mr Nightingale is a Vague, and he's accepted the fact ever since he caught himself saying thankyou to a ticket machine in the London Underground. Mr Nightingale says, "We Vagues are an oppressed minority. We're oppressed by the vivid and the competent. Only if you're a Vague yourself can you know how all pervasive vagueism is in British society. Daily we're submitted to such flagrantly vaguest remarks as… 'Where do you think you're going?' And 'Wake up, Jack',… all for something we can't help, because we were born that way." He's right. And if he were ever to organise a conference, and if any of us remembered to attend, and we weren't arrested on the way, then I suggest… well, whatever it was I was going to suggest.

For we Vagues vagueness is a way of life. Arguably we should receive some sort of state benefit because we're liable to an attack twenty-four hours a day. And it can be just as costly in the privacy of one's own home. A couple of days ago I was painting in water colour. My wife kindly brought me a cup of tea. Quarter of an hour later there was alarm in the house. It was thought I might be haemorrhaging, but forensic tests revealed merely (merely! the entire family and the cat required *arnica* for shock) that I'd rinsed a brushful of alizarin crimson in my tea-mug. My wife very generously gave me another mug of tea and suggested I try not to do it again. I did try. When ten minutes later I ran moaning into the kitchen it was with an issue, corpse-blue, pumping from the side of my mouth. This time I'd taken a gulp from the right mug… the one I used to rinse my brushes in.

Some people think that vagueness has to do with the aging process. This typifies the vagueist prejudice that we Vagues have to contend with. *Vagus nascitur, non fit.* And I can prove it. For instance that time I was sixteen, travelling in the underground with my sister. My sister was quite something. She was older than I, a fashion model, and all decked out for work. At the first stop an impressive man, almost certainly a brigadier, with white groomed whiskers and a Guards' tie, came aboard. I knew at once what would make his day... a crisp show of respect, proof that the young could still produce a touch of swagger. I leapt to my feet. "Sir," I said, "Please, my seat, I insist." "Good chap," he said, and sat beside my sister. Away we rumbled. After a few moments I stole a modest glance at the pair of them. I suppose I expected some accolade from their expressions of pride. Not so. My sister was wearing that older sister expression. And as for the brigadier, he was clearly intent on having a stroke. I had just time to think, "the old dog, I bet he tried to pinch her," when he struggled up, scorched me in passing with an, "I'll be damned if I do," and stormed off down the train. It was then I saw the problem. Apart from my sister and myself, the entire carriage had been empty.

Research shows that undergrounds and railways are an environment in which Vagues are especially vulnerable. For instance, it was on Exeter station I suffered recently the experience that converted me to vague militancy. I was travelling to Berkshire for a big golf match, and as sometimes happens the nerves were getting to me. I did what any sensible person would do in these circumstances, and my clubs over my shoulder and suitcase in hand was just re-emerging onto the platform when I noticed I was carrying under my arm the almost intact roll of lavatory paper. So I went to put it back. Of course the door of the closet had slammed... I was faced with the outlay of an additional 2p. I stood for a moment pondering the way in which the honest and the reliable are penalised by society, when I noticed there was a gap of two or three inches under the door. That was the answer. The Gents was deserted... no problem. I got down on my hands and knees and, my clubs still over my shoulder, my suitcase beside me, began to work the roll under the door. It was a tight fit, and I can only say that it required character, determination and a good deal of strength. The operation almost complete, I paused to get my breath and it was then I sensed someone was watching me. If you've ever tried to find an official on Exeter station you too will know it's a lost cause. But now I can tell you where you'll find one. Lurking somewhere out of sight at the back of the Gents' loo, no doubt detailed to harass the unsuspecting Vague. It was the unbridled suspicion, the uniformed glare of this official, as I accelerated past him on tiptoe, that finally decided me it was time to move onto the offensive.

Mr Nightingale is right. What we need is an organisation. Vagues against Punctuality, Incisiveness and Discipline, or VAPID. "VAPID," he says, "will harass newspapers which continue to use vagueist expressions, like wool-gathering or dozy, and will try to persuade the *Guardian* to institute a weekly Vague's page with an even higher proportion of misprints than usual. We want vaguer business, a vaguer Britain, and indeed a vaguer world. A vaguer world, we say, is a safer world. After all, who's going to press that button if he's lost the instruction manual which tells him which one it is?"

Attaboy, Mr Nightjar. I'm right behind you.

Issue 104 - May/June 1984

GOOD SCHOOLING

THE HEADMASTER OF my boarding preparatory school wore a monocle which meant of course we called him Pop-eye. But *sotto voce* because, a retired major, he carried a temper the mere threat of which would sting the eyes like mustard gas. Which isn't to say that he was short on strength. We knew this from having been on the receiving end of a formidable piddlywink. Nights before leave-outs he would visit us in our dormitories. At the sound of his approach even the bravest of us would blanche - which was precisely the signal Pop-eye was watching for. "Can't have your parents see you looking off-colour," he'd say, and he'd grab someone's cheek between his thumb and knuckle and squeeze. "That's better, now you look in the pink. Now let's see, anyone else for piddlywinks?"

After a dose of piddlywinks it was important that Pop-eye didn't see one blubbing. I think the thought that any boy in his school should ever blub incensed him. The time he caught me blubbing he was particularly incensed because up until that moment he had expected great things. My father had been killed in action which was something Pop-eye definitely approved of. This meant that what chiefly he expected from me was bags of guts and an eye for the ultimate sacrifice. When I blubbed after the piddlywinks he gave me the look that to this day is probably responsible for the problem I have with blushing. Though possibly this would be better attributed to effects of repeated piddlywinks on the vascular system in my cheeks.

At Sandhurst Pop-eye had been a year senior to Monty. There were two men Monty had respect for - a grudging respect for Rommel who put up a decent show in the desert, and like every other man and boy an ungrudging respect tinged with blue abject funk for Pop-eye. I know this because Monty used to spend his leaves at my preparatory school with Mr and Mrs Pop-eye. Which merely served to intensify the effects of a decent education.

My first day at school was May 8th 1945, which happened to be V.E. Day. The school was paraded in three ranks in front of the flag to be told the news. Something in Pop-eye's voice told even a new squit that this was unlikely to be cause for rejoicing. Too true. This budding manhood, tragically cut off before its prime from a decent opportunity for the ultimate sacrifice, spent the rest of the morning marching around the sand playground, singing Lily Marlene, presumably, though the point was at the time lost on me, in emulation of the Desert Rats. Pop-eye had decided that

Monty's war had merited a triumph, and that next time he came on leave the school would put on a show for him.

The sand playground engagement was an inglorious affair. I was placed one from the end of the line, in front of the other new squit whose father, a dentist, had failed to achieve the ultimate sacrifice. Pop-eye's worst fears were probably realised when this boy showed he was unable to march. He was one of those troopers who led with the left arm and left leg together. And, boy, did he do it with conviction! If it was his foot he was in step with, then his hand would catch mine a painful thwack on the knuckles. But if he was in step with his arms then he'd tread on my heel and the two of us would go down in the sand as if felled by mortar fire. The first two or three times Pop-eye turned a blind monocle. Finally it was too much for him. We were sent to our classroom and spent the rest of the morning learning a poem, some of the lines of which I've never forgotten:

In an age of fops and toys,
Want of wisdom, void of right,
Who will aid heroic boys
To hazard all for freedom's fight?
Break sharply off their jolly games
For sake of comrades gay
And quit proud homes and youthful dames
For famine, toil and fray.

I don't think there is anything sinister about that third from last line, anymore than the incident when on a summer night Field-Marshal Montgomery of Alamein came tip-toeing into our dormitory. Reduced to the ranks he put up a brave show in the ensuing pillow-fight until... until the sound of Pop-eye's jackboots were heard in the corridor. In a trice Monty was behind the door. "Any man sneaking on me," he barked, "I'll have him cashiered." The door flung open. "Own up!" explodes Pop-eye. Even when in the clear it was best to own up - the alternative was unimaginable. "Down to my study," says Pop-eye, "And bring the spoon." The wooden spoon, four to six strokes with the flat or the round, was reserved for dormitory offences. For some ceremonial reason it was kept on top of the cupboard in the dormitory passage. The culprit, carrying the spoon, would proceed to the study. In the tender days following he'd find opportunity to sneak to the cupboard and inscribe name and number of strokes on the head of the spoon.

As we shuffled in our slippers towards the door we were of course wondering - was Monty about to do the decent thing? If not he was making a mistake he never made with Rommel - he was underrating the opposition. Pop-eye could detect failure to own up through the six-foot walls of a bunker. Suddenly he snatched the door and swung it shut. The memory of Monty in defeat is not easy to live with. Probably I should have kept it to myself. Presently Pop-eye said: "Back to bed you lot. As for you, you follow me." Which is what Monty did.

Next day, in first break, while the others kept *cave*, I went behind lines to that cupboard. But Monty's name wasn't there on the spoon. Possibly he hadn't known where it was kept. I hope that's the explanation. Because if he wormed his way out a hiding then I reckon someone had better start writing an alternative history of the 20th Century.

Issue 118 - September/October 1986

WAITING FOR THE CALL

I'VE NEVER BEEN modest about what seems to me my unique qualification to become *Resurgence's* first sports editor. Put simply it is this - a compulsive and entirely neurotic preoccupation with the outcome of virtually every competition. On wet days I can reduce myself to centre-court fever watching a show-down sprint between a couple of rain-drops on a window-pane. It is not a propensity that, in my experience, makes me a restful person to live with, but it does equip one with an informed point-of-view.

For instance how many of you readers would, unaided, have realised that what lies beneath the British Political System is not the electorate's interest in prescription charges or small school education - but adherence to the ancient ritual of 'first past the post'. What we proudly refer to as the Democratic Prerogative is nothing more or less than the right to a free ticket in one of the biggest sweepstakes in the Sporting Calendar. And if you doubt this I suggest you make a study of the dates chosen for general elections. Never during Wimbledon or the climax to the football season. Thursday is a favourite choice - but never the Thursday of the Lords Test. You see *they* know. I won't overstate it by saying they know it *consciously*, because as sportspeople manqués they're of course not conscious of anything very much. But they do have this sporting instinct and so realise that if they are to achieve anything like a decent gate they must avoid competition with the real crowd-pullers.

The present crisis in British Politics, as any who tuned into the recent Party conference must have noticed, is a pervasive sense of non-event. Whether it's Christians or Lions or blow-football, you can't get the game under way if everyone's on the same side. It's a real problem, and it's bringing the game into disrepute. You don't have to be an Oliver Cromwell in green spectacles to see that these players are having the devil of a time getting on opposite sides of the net. No, that understates it - the current problem is finding four sides to an inherently one-sided net. When the only live motion is the one they don't table, namely "That this house should look to the alternative," we understand that we're dealing with four parties (plus umpteen ministries and a trades union movement) of conservatives. What we want is our ball-game back.

There's another problem. Is a political system which, at election time, reduces all parties to the level of foot-of-the-table teams fighting against relegation to the second division - is it likely to throw up the kind of leadership sane, law-abiding people would want to live with? Football managers, with their ability to countenance falling gates, hooliganism on the terraces, to hold their own in the boardroom cross-fire, and with their fanatical concern with results - no doubt they're good solid citizens but hardly the leadership material recommended by the Tao Te Ching:

I take no action and people are reformed.
I enjoy peace and people become honest.
I do nothing and people become rich.
I have no desires and people return/ to the good and simple life.

It's odd that an age so in awe of pragmatism, and so obsessed with the results as they come off the teleprinter, should be subject to a political system where the fact of having achieved office is the demonstrable disqualification of the right to govern.

To solve this leadership crisis maybe we've got to get back to the sort of system operating around Rome in the 5th Century B.C. This, you'll remember, was the system that brought Cincinnatus into the limelight. Listen carefully. Cincinatus was informed, as he ploughed his field, that the senate had chosen him dictator. Upon this he left his ploughed land with regret, and repaired to the field of battle. He conquered the enemy and returned to Rome in triumph; and sixteen days after his appointment he laid down his office, and retired back to plough his fields. In his 80th year he was again summoned as dictator, and after a successful campaign he resigned the absolute power he had enjoyed only 21 days, nobly disregarding the rewards that were offered him by the senate, and once more returned to his farm. Beautiful - the purest green, and I bet his technology was appropriate to boot. You see a true leader doesn't want the job. It's what we sports editors call the Mike Brearley factor - appoint a philosophy don as skipper and you regain the ashes. The only other parallel in modern history to the Cincinnatus episode is the time they slapped a pair of pads on Bishop David Shepherd, sent him out to open the innings against the Aussies, and he made a ton. I should think Jonathon Porritt's been making a study of Cincinnatus, as well as green provision for a statue of him to be erected in Parliament Square. What we should do is institute the annual Cincinnatus Lectures. I mustn't forget to tell the Editor.

Incidentally I've noticed a marked improvement in Satish since his pilgrimage. The other day he said to me, "Why don't you do a Didymus piece on golf courses?" I held my breath. Was he going to offer me the sports editorship there and then? He went on to say that during his pilgrimage he'd walked across some beautiful golf courses, and that the members had been very helpful in showing him the way. I was amazed. In my experience golf club members are about as welcoming as medieval barons. The only time they've ever shown me the way it's been in no uncertain terms. Anyway I judge that editorial attitude towards a sports page is definitely softening. Meantime I keep in trim. I tell myself I don't want the job. I eschew all concern with results - apart from the essential hour of Sports Report at 5pm on Saturday afternoons. When the call comes I intend it shall be as a complete surprise. What's more he's going to have to look to me. Like Cincinnatus, I'll be up in the garden, dosing the slugs.

Issue 120 - January/February 1987

FLANNELLING

IN MY VIEW readers are likely to vote this one of the half-dozen outstanding Didymus contributions to the emergent consciousness. Occasionally one does hear *Resurgence* criticised for swanning about in circles in a mystical twilight. These critics are usually steely boffin-eyed persons who wouldn't know a circle dance from a Dashing White Sergeant. If I'm cornered by one of these characters I give them the glare treatment, let them know what their view has confessed…that they've been skipping Didymus. And here, embracing as it does the intermediately technological, the human scale, energy and raw material conservation, personal growth potential, is the piece to prove it.

It's depressing that once again Research and Development of a

British invention required American backing, but at least the personnel were homespun. My wife and I were touring the Rocky Mountains somewhere west of Denver. In a bar a cowboy who was old enough to have known better congratulated us on arriving just when the grizzly bears were waking up ravenous and with a bad hang-over. We decided we'd not camp the first night, and so set out into the wilderness to find an appropriate small-scale motel.

We found this in the clouds near a small township called Rollinsville. Run by a woman with her feet in the Earth, and consciousness that had the elevated, giddy quality of a hang-glider…a potential *Resurgence* reader if ever I saw one. It was while we were registering that she declared her hand. A sensitive, a pendulum artist and a dowser of metals…and we were lucky to have caught her because she'd been on her way out for an evening's psychic panning up near the snow-line.

"Ah," I said smoothly, "there's psychic gold in them hills."

"There ain't," she said giving me the kind of withering look that only sensitives of the Annie Oakley school can command.

"But they're sure as hell ticking with u-ranium."

She chucked us a key, and we were left to get on with it.

Our room, like so many that have given roof to really important discoveries, was in an unpromising shed round the back. There was an involuntary simplicity about the place, and a kind of on-the-frontier disregard for furbishment that seemed to suggest the big strike in the hills was overdue. One instance of this was the towelling provision. There wasn't. What we were given were two face flannels.

"Well," I remember thinking, "the frontier's the frontier, and it's necessary that I take a shower."

Necessity, as we all know, is the mother of invention.

Recklessly I grabbed one of the flannels and used it for washing. How in that chill mountain air I was to dry myself was a problem I would confront in due course. And in that due course I was privileged to make the following invention.

Towels are bad for drying. A dry towel is not disposed to getting itself wet. A dry towel does not absorb water as readily as a damp towel. I realised this statement could try the credulity of even a regular *Resurgence* subscriber (another reason why we Didymus authors are reassured to have on board the more wired-up readership from *Undercurrents*). Yes, but then with a damp towel you are not going to get perfectly dry. No matter what acreage the towel, before you're dry the towel is damp and that damp precludes a dry finish. It is terrible to think of the sub-continents of hemp or sisal or whatever one makes towels with, and the concommitant centuries of native exploitation that have gone to producing even bigger, deeper pile, ineffective towels. And when one thinks of the steam-laundering this has involved one can only marvel at the relative constancy of the polar ice-caps.

And what all along was all that was needed?

Two flannels. One damp. One dry. The procedure is as follows. First a thorough wipe-down with the damp flannel…with every now and then, after say a leg or a…well anyway every now and then you stop and wring out the water. You'll be astonished by two things, (a) by how much water you wring out with each wringing and (b) by how dry this quick wipe-down leaves you. All that now remains is for you to buff yourself up with the dry flannel, a quick finish which even at sea-level I find energises the skin and leaves a natural flush the allure of which is, in my experience, pretty well irresistible.

Which reminds me, my wife also took a shower and, with those two identical flannels, exhaustively confirmed my findings. Which suggests we may have here something in the category of the Scotsman's teabag...in other words two flannels could probably service an entire expedition.

Intermediate technology at its purest, incalculable conservation of natural resources and non-renewable fuels, self-reliance, job-satisfaction...and never again the traveller's phobia of being caught in the outback without a decent-sized towel. All this for the price of an ancillary face-flannel.

An alternative Nobel Prize? Not if our landlady were one of the panel. I tried to explain the invention to her next morning as we checked out. Sensitive she may have been, but here was something beyond her range. Clearly rattled she gave a muffled cuss and then as if to prove a point produced from a cupboard beside the reception desk two gigantic mustard-coloured towels.

Issue 124 - September/October 1987

SHARING THE JOKE

THEY'RE RIGHT, Mrs Thatcher's political judgement is uncanny. Look at her timing of the General Election. Not for the first time the announcement comes the day after a *Resurgence* deadline. Didymus gagged, condemned to the sideline, again unable to have anything but a marginal influence on the outcome.

What I would have hammered home to the electorate was Mrs T's constant reiteration (and so that of leading members of her male chorus) that nuclear weapons have kept the peace in Europe for more than forty years. I would have implored the more superficial commentators from the green fringe to take her passionate declaration to heart. Wars are declared by politicians, and among politicians Mrs Thatcher is pre-eminent. So Mrs Thatcher would know. She was clearly warning us: Remove the constraint of the Bomb and the next day the conventional forces of Thatcherism will march on…well, why not Moscow? I for one am prepared to take her very seriously.

Forty years. I suppose it has been peaceful, has it?

Primo Levi in his book *The Truce*, which describes the six months it took him to get home to Italy after being released by the Russians from Auschwitz, gives us an astonishing sense of the confused war-zone after the end of hostilities. We feel all the contributing energies; martial, racial, political, national, sectarian, those of fear, vengeance and unspent rage, and perhaps above all that of cold abstract ideology - were all suddenly awry, all in a vacuum, all racing to regroup, claim identity again within the only constitution that offered them coherence; that of authorised militant enmity. So perhaps Mrs Thatcher really was correct that nuclear weapons have suppressed the manifestation that is war. But the real point is that whatever *status quo* they may or may not have achieved, it's neither accurate nor very useful to call it peace.

None of this was Levi's concern. He was writing about his journey home. It is proof of his stature as a writer that in so doing he illuminates just about everything that is positive and negative in humanity. Because his eye, even after all he had suffered, was still simple, and because almost certainly his seeing was love, his was the balanced view. Philip Roth assesses Levi's account of his time in Auschwitz, in *If This Is A Man*: "one of the century's truly necessary books". I'd agree. Primo Levi was a peace-maker. And in as much as the peace he worked for was genuine peace, he and his work shed a light in which both our stockpile of bombs and the shadow in us which they express, can be seen for precisely what they are.

For two reasons I've wanted Didymus to honour Levi. First,

that he died early last year. There are a few who when they die leave the rest of us feeling unprotected, feeling that our whole basis for hope is suddenly more vulnerable. It eases the worry to share it. If you don't know what I'm talking about, and haven't read his books, then please, that's what you should do.

Second, he was one of the most humorous of writers. Funny, the recorder of Auschwitz! Recently I was having a meal alone in a bistro, and reading the new paperback edition of *The Truce*. I'd come on a description that had me rocking with laughter. Self-consciously I glanced up, and saw a couple sitting at the next table staring at me uneasily. I realised then they'd seen the cover of this book I was finding so much of a tickle. Sepia, black and white, the grim, starving image of a line of Auschwitz prisoners standing beyond the barbed wire. I tried to wipe the smile off my face, but I think I'd already ruined their meal.

The passage was only a few pages on from one of the book's most horrifying descriptions of an Auschwitz sick-ward, an unspeakable mortuary from which Levi rescued his friend Cesare. But now he's at a transit camp on the way home. He's playing a football match refereed by a wonderful, crazy camp official, a kind of Russian Monsieur Hulot. It's a needle match, Italians versus Poles, and the referee is determined to stamp his authority on the game. It's difficult to illustrate humour out of context, but here's a flavour:

At other times, when the referee managed to get the ball at his feet, he would make everybody move away, and would kick it at the goal with all his strength; then he would turn radiantly to the public, which bellowed with anger, and salute it for a long time, clasping his hands above his head like a victorious boxer. He was, however, rigorously impartial.

I don't know what humour is, but it does seem a property of, or perhaps a subversive agent in the cause of, sanity. Levi doesn't go out of his way to be funny, but as with everything else, if he sees something funny he'll record it. What one sees depends on the capacity of one's eye - to be funny one must be able to see the joke. And if the joke is there, that is the life-proof of its propriety.

Levi's appetite for looking, and the sense of balance that his looking achieves, suggest an eye of almost unbelievable capacity. Because his eye never cops out on anything, it propounds the absolute abiding fact and necessity of freedom.

As a matter of fact I wouldn't want to deny Mrs Thatcher's commitment to freedom - some version of it. But the problem is, that commitment where there is not the fullest capacity to see becomes all too easily just another of those stones that pave the way to hell. Commitment that is political judgement, that is what the world suffers.

Primo Levi said:

"I prefer the role of witness to that of judge. I can bear witness only to things which I myself endured and saw."

In my political judgement, such a man is qualified to govern. And there's another thing he said, which I'd like handed out at every party conference:

"In every part of the world, wherever you begin by denying the fundamental liberties of humankind, and equality among people, you move towards the concentration camp system, and it is a road on which it is difficult to halt."

For those of keen political judgement I should perhaps point out - he wasn't joking.

Issue 126 - January/February 1988

AFTER THOUGHT

I'M JOLLY GRATEFUL to the reader who tore a strip off me (see letters, issue 126) for reducing my wife's allure after a two-flannel bluff to a mere afterthought. Quite right. And this very properly reintroduces the question too long ignored in this column - the whole question of Fourth World provisions for minority rights.

I must say straight away that I'm disappointed with the Welsh. And I'm not referring here to the contempt with which they persistently treat an apparent minority of Englishmen on the rugby field (perhaps I should be since I hear the undercurrent of readers saying the *Resurgence* Sports Page is another issue kept too long in the cupboard).

No, my graver concern is with their treatment, inexplicable after all they've been submitted to over the centuries, of a salient minority. A minority that is truly representative. And one which is, in my view, unlikely to just go away. I mean we Vagues.

I was on a Vagues' work retreat in a cottage near Carmarthen - with in fact Fairfax, our poetry editor. We'd gone into town to shop and, not at all as an afterthought, to post a letter to my wife. In fact it was to the Post Office we went first, where we received deceptively tolerant treatment. It was later, in the grocer's, that things began to go badly. Eager to pay, I reached into my jacket pocket for the wallet that held our kitty-money - and produced the letter I had just posted to my wife. Fairfax it was who went straight to the heart of the mystery. But then he's had any amount of relevant experience. Like the time he planted the packet of assorted spring flowers, given him by his aunt for Christmas, in the bed outside his study window. When in August they'd still not appeared he was unable to contain his sense of injury. He tackled his aunt. That's when she invented the one-liner that has become something of a catch-phrase among those Vagues who are able to remember it: "You planted it outside the window - what an odd thing to do with a packet of bath salts."

The grocer watched my consultation with Fairfax, warily. When at length I waved the envelope at him, and explained that I'd posted my wallet, he put our groceries out of reach behind the counter. He then cast me the look so wounding to Vagues and to the members of other minorities.

The postmaster was still less sympathetic. I think he thought I was from the militant wing, serving him a crypto-message that I'd planted a bomb in his box. He looked as if he was in two minds about whether to clear the building. Then he did…of us. He told us we had to wait for the postman who made the collection. I don't' want to make too much of this, but I suspect he was passing the buck.

The postman wasn't very sympathetic either. Even though I took pains to explain politely - which takes some doing when one's spent the last three hours walking penniless around Carmarthen with Fairfax who's out of fags. I said, "Excuse me, but our kitty's in there."

The postman, who looked like Moriarty (I mean the Welsh rugby player), said, "How did it get there?"

I waved my wife's letter at him and said, "I posted it."

It's when that deafening look comes from someone of the stature of Moriarty that one's thankful for VAPID. Vagues Against Precision, Incisiveness and ... No I can't remember what it stands for. But to be honest it doesn't have much muscle. Not in Wales anyway. And now I come to think of it, maybe I'm wrong about the Welsh. From what I've heard of Lloyd George and Taliesin, one or two of the things they got up to sound pretty vague. Then (and I hope this won't sound like another afterthought) there was my wife's mother. She was Welsh, and she once did a U-turn on the motorway. On reflection I feel pretty sure that the seat of the discrimination lies in the heart of the Post Office.

So now I've decided to take matters into my own hands. I'm going to quit being so vague. It's no longer worth it. Not since last September when I was forced into glasses. If the time I've spent looking for my specs were placed end to end I'd now be a good twenty years younger.

Today is Ash Wednesday, and I'm giving up losing my glasses for Lent. It's the way to achieve something big. Don't try to be indiscriminately non-vague - you'll do yourself an injury. A small focused beginning is the answer. That way one will transmute a habit of frailty into the strength of corrective discipline. Forty days and forty nights there'll not be a moment I can't tell you precisely where my glasses are. Right now they're on my nose. But if I were out in the garden and you asked me, I'd be able to say, "My glasses are where I left them. My glasses are..." Yes well, I'll report back. I'm confident that it's out of such small beginnings that we achieve a universal one-pointedness. It wouldn't surprise me if by mid-summer I wasn't the chairman of Mensa.

Oh, and just one afterthought. My wife also wears glasses. She also loses them. I would like to say that when this happens - when the whole house is again turned upside-down; and we're late, and running in circles, and it's her glasses we're all looking for - I find it *equally*, no I would concede even a shade more, infuriating.

Issue 128 - May/June 1988

VAGUELY GREEN

I **WAS DEEPLY** affected by the readers' unprecedented response to my fiftieth Didymus piece. One can feel lonely out here on the margins of sanity, but, knowing there are people prepared to weigh one's arguments to the milligram, it does make it all worthwhile. One strenuous letter pointed out that the line from Dame Vera's *White Cliffs of Dover* upon which I'd based my entire apodixis was a misquotation. Good, well done. The other, revealing a discipleship I'd never have counted on, that I'd miscounted. It wasn't the fiftieth, it was still only the forty-ninth. Brought tears to my eyes, that did.

Bah! when did I ever suggest you get to be "an unacknowledged legislator of the world" by slavish adherence to verifiable fact? So *this* is the fiftieth, is it? Let's get on with it then. I know, let's (since everyone else seems to be) have a go at Mrs Thatcher.

Yesterday was the European election. The result won't be known till Sunday, but to the informed observer it's already clear that the Greens have romped to power. So where did Mrs Thatcher get it wrong? There are some things which only one's best friend...etc. Best friend? Yes, you see ever since the greening of the Thatcher complexion it's becoming increasingly clear that some wild new influence is abroad in Number 10. It would be ludicrous to suggest that Mrs T is yet ready for the *Resurgence* Classified Ads section. But something hectoring in the tone of that letter about Dame Vera suggested to me that Didymus has the ear of the presidium.

In which case, let us proceed obliquely.

I would say that one of the things preventing Mrs T from making further inexplicable headway with the electorate is her declaration that the world could not conceivably hold together without the bondage of nuclear bombs. It is, I think, beginning to dawn on even her new, carefully-contrived, share-holding majority that no one in her right mind would choose to stick with the bomb if it weren't that she was, in a personal sense, sitting on something in the order of 3,000 megatons of TNT, and properly afraid to move. From a personal-growth point of view this sort of equation is elementary; the sort of thing which at a Zurich kindergarten you find discussed at assembly.

Further, knowing what we do about armament projections, we can confidently assert that her explosive inner equilibrium is, because of her unique position, projected not where might properly be expected (i.e. on Dennis's stable visage) but on firstly the convenient Lower House, an image of the divided psyche if ever there was one, and thence on the broader features of the world at large. How does this very personal condition get translated into Tory Policy? Like this. "God knows what would happen if I tried to dismantle the bomb! The bomb therefore must be seen as the safeguard of peace. Without the threat of the bomb all life is inconceivable. The bomb is something humankind must learn to live with. Since I *am* the bomb I'm something else they'd better learn to live with. If no one rocks the boat I should just about have enough grip to see the bomb doesn't go off." In other words, a divided world is pre-required by Mrs T's conviction that it's she who's in control.

If you travel, before long you begin to meet people who don't altogether want to be under Mrs T's control. People who are daring to think a divided world doesn't really add up when there's only, for instance, the one ozone layer. People who have more uplifting things to spend their money on than even armaments.

I'm just back from Russia, which means I know what I'm talking about. The Russian people are not entirely sure what to make of Mrs Thatcher but, like many of us in the West, are anxious about her state of mind. I know this because I went out of my way to conduct the relevant research. And by out of the way I mean a long way out of my way. In Tashkent. In an attempt to walk across town to the Museum of Applied Art. Like most people I'd always thought Tashkent was two or three palm trees, a few camels, a jug of wine and thou. It isn't, it's the fourth largest city in the Soviet Union. I'd been walking some hours when finally I persuaded a taxi driver to take a chance with me. Together we consulted my map for a time. He looked at me once or twice, as if I were part of a package that didn't add up, and then we were off. Slowly. There was barely room for two of us in the little old car, which he didn't steer but nudged along the road like a novice at the helm of a yacht.

He was a solemn man, and he seemed a little on edge. One time he scowled and his eyebrows came together in a fair imitation of Stalin's moustache. He asked me something. "Angliski," I replied, hoping this would explain. I think it did. I think it explained a lot. He glanced at me with, I now realise, the suspicion I could be certifiable not solely on my own account, but also by association. Preoccupied he looked back at the road which to judge by his white-knuckled grip on the wheel was becoming increasingly choppy.

Quite suddenly he groaned, took both hands from the wheel, clenched them, and began to beat the sides of his head just above his ears. "A berserk kalmuk," I thought, and felt for the handle of the door. It was then he opened his mouth and, syllable by syllable, gave vent to this extraordinary sound. "MAR-R-GAR-R-RET TCHAT-TCHAR." His expression seemed to be saying, "Now that... *that* is something else." I know how he felt.

We never did make the Museum of Applied Art. After a while I saw we were passing my hotel, and we decided to call it a day. Actually the pair of us had done pretty well. Particularly when you consider that the map hadn't been a great deal of help. What it had been, as I later discovered, was the map of Samarkand.

Issue 136 - September/October 1989

The Great Tax REFORM!

I **WASN'T SURPRISED** to get the editor's call asking for the Didymus alternative to the Poll Tax. In fact I'd already done my homework.

A holistic approach of course - from now on we'll have only the one tax.

The card

Everyone to carry what's called an Exchequer Card. I'm afraid for the foreseeable future this will have to be plastic. I regret also that the system relies on a computer - but one quite unlike those you find nowadays under green wraps in so many leading alternative homes, in other words a simple one.

On each card will be found an embossed number of this general order:

95372074 3 31

The first 8 figure number is for individual identification purposes. Each person has his or her individual number. The cards are non-counterfeitable (if you can't yourself figure how this may be ensured I suggest you contact one of our readers who was previously a subscriber to Undercurrents).

The second single figure (in this case 3) is the benefit grade code. 1 is standard, i.e. no benefit. 2 is Pensioner. 3 is Single Parent. 4 is unemployed. And do on.

The third two-figure number (in this case 31) is the

person's Local Authority code. Every Local Authority in the land has its own number.

The Till

Every trader of whatever commodity or service will be provided with a cash till specifically equipped. Considering that videorecorders, fax machines, word-processors are now standard accessories in the home. I don't see this provision of tills poses any serious problem. When the charge for any purchase is rung up on one of these tills the customer's card is inserted in a special slot - the machine then, quick as a shot, calculates the total cost including the central exchequer tax *and* the relevant local authority percentage charge. The trader collects the full sum; and the till keeps record of the trader's sale, the tax, at prescribed rate, due to the exchequer, and the local authority's charge. The local authority's coded number will ensure it collects its due from its subscribers whether or not they purchase within it's area.

Pricing

The price of every commodity or service is prefixed by one of four letters, each denoting a distinct category.

A, The Essential (Bread, milk, electricity, etc.).

B, The Staple (postage, petrol, cheese, string, etc.)

C, The Luxury (wine, CDs, second homes, golf clubs, Gentleman's Relish, etc.)

D, Super Luxury (aeroplanes, privatised number plates, private armies, third homes etc.)

The price is also suffixed by one of four letters, and again each denotes a distinct but related category.

E, for a product or service that is environmentally acceptable, or whose manufacture or pursuit relies on craft-skill and/or appropriate technology.

F, for so-called standard products and services.

G, for exploitative products.

H, for criminally exploitative products.

Each prefix and suffix will make, according to the discretion or conceit of the Chancellor, its own adjustment to the tax total. No administrative problem - an instruction to the central computer will be communicated instantly to every till in the country. State of the Art. No problem.

The Chancellor

Frankly, this doesn't leave the Chancellor a lot to do.

First he (that's fair, isn't it? I don't think any woman's been tempted to take on this job) decides on the tax rate payable by the respective benefit grades. Let's say - and I want it clear that these are his ideas, not mine:

1. Standard   20%
2. Pensioner   10%
3. Single Parent   5%
4. Unemployed   Zero

(Incidentally all benefits can now be collected from local cash-machines by using one's designated Exchequer Card and PIN number - which does away with 3 million bureaucrats and reduces the overall tax demand to virtually nil).

He then, according to the colour of his politics, decides on the ratio of 'quality' taxation levels. Let's say:

A (Essential)	5%
B (Staple)	10%
C (Luxury)	20%
D (Super-luxury)	50%
E (Green, craft, AT)	10%
F (Standard)	Zero
G (Exploitative)	50%
H (Criminally exploitative)	100%

And then all he has to do is calculate the total income from tax the Exchequer requires. The Local Authorities will have let him know their demands - their money collected centrally is merely channelled to them, their budgeting is separate and autonomous, and they thus remain wholly accountable to their constituents. This total figure simply arrived at (our Editor would do it on the back of an envelope), is fed to the computer. The Chancellor presses the button. A couple of micro-seconds and the computer will have told him the score, he will know precisely the related tax levels, standard and otherwise, that are required to balance his budget.

In Practice

No, on the contrary it is extremely simple. A couple of examples will show you.
1. A Pensioner from Gloucestershire (Card No. 52438721 2 21) buying a loaf of wholemeal bread correctly priced A.82E, will be charged:

Trader price	.82
+ 5% for A rating	.041
-10% for E rating	-.082
+10% for benefit grade rating 2	.082
+10% for Local Authority charge	.082
Total (rounded up to nearest p)	.94

Of which 82p goes to the trader, 4p to the central exchequer and 8p to the Local Authority.

And all that will have been worked out in a flash the moment the price is rung up and the purchaser's card inserted in the till - if you doubt it, go and have a look at the latest machines they have in Tesco.

No more tax demands. At the moment of purchase the tax has all been paid.

2. A Business executive from Virginia Water (Card No. 94774550 1 78) buying a microwave oven correctly priced C500.00G will be charged:

Trader price	500.00
+ 20% for C rating	100.00
+ 50% for G rating	250.00
+ 20% for nil benefit rating 1	100.00
+ 12% for Local Authority charge	60.00
Total	1,010.00

Of which £500.00 goes to the trader, £450.00 goes to the central exchequer, £60.00 goes to the local authority and Bob's your uncle.

A Few General Notes

Industry and manufacturing will of course be taxed the same way. The industry, just as an individual, will have its own Exchequer Card, and will pay for what it buys (power and raw materials and so forth). The Chancellor is free to set or revise, or use to penalise or give incentive, the level of tax any bracket or size or mode of industry should pay - after all he has the whole alphabet to play with.

Charities to be zero rated.

Books to receive an extraordinary concession.

But overall the glory of this system is not only its simplicity (a fool might have thought of it), but the freedom it gives the Chancellor to really express himself, and to change his mind whenever he likes. Policy is implemented by the merest 'tweak' of the buttons. Concessions, benefits, incentives, penalties, either to groups of individuals or industries, all can be readily introduced.

If at the end of the month the Exchequer's short of a bob, if the PM on impulse has bought 1,000 new Tridents, if policy dictates the government should be knocking the hell out of the pensioners, or shifting a mountain of mad-cow beef, or giving a tax concession on wine to regular columnists, if the Greens have seized power and decided to boost the organics industry - why, the Chancellor just 'tweaks' a button and the central computer communicates his fine tuning to every till in the land.

When you post a copy of this to your MP, I should send it first class. We need to move fast. I'm told that in Eastern Europe there's currently a good deal of interest in the best of *Resurgence* thinking. It's a damn shame when good British inventions, like the hovercraft, get taken overseas, and aren't given the proper backing at home. There is however one drawback, and about this I think it's important we come clean. Loose bureaucrats. This new system is going to put so many civil servants out of a job that the resulting saving to the Inland Revenue could, if my early predictions are correct, do away with the need for taxation altogether. However, what on Earth we're going to do with all these surplus civil servants is a real headache. Personally I suggest... no, come on, I can't be expected to solve all the problems. Here's one I'll just have to leave to the Editor.

Issue 142 - September/October 1990

The Consice Version of
THE *RESURGENCE* BARK
or ATTENTION ALL SHIPPING

(Written for Resurgence 25th anniversary)

Down in the local harbour,
Was putting out to sea
Part organ and part oracle,
A sort of appropriate coracle,
The latest technology.

Captain Papworth swore from the poop,
"A pox on your detergence!
You think that's the way to beat the slick?
What you need's a drum of *Resurgence*."

Up on the bridge was a cobbler's shop
(by the way the sun was still growing darker);
Requisitioned from British Coal,
He could cobble us all a quick re-sole
This ingenious Schumacher.

And beside his bench a fabulous beast
From his basket started to stir
Half man, half lion, half half-shorn hound,
Such was the Leo Polled Kohr.

On the fo'c'sle hatchcover they hatched a plot
Efficient as nuclear fissioncy:
In time we all came to Seymour and more
The good sense in Self-sufficiency.

Almost over the bar when they struck a rock
The boat was headed under:
The skipper had been relieved of his post
By President Kaunda.

Where would a new pilot ever be found
Who could handle our protean barge...
Of course! I know, the Edgware Road:
He's the Karma of the Raj.

"Now where are we headed?" the crew all yelled,
"Could it be the China Station?"
But the dusky helmsman closed his eyes
And breathed, "No Destination."

"Hold on tight!" our admiral announced.
"You may think I'm just a late-Kumar,
But the minds and pockets I intend to pick
Should soon have scotched that rumar.

"We'll sail due West down the mighty M4
Our course set green for heaven,
Meaning this diversion into (deepest) Wales
Should earn us the visa for Devon."

With that the Green Ensign was hoisted,
The crew gave a rapturous cheer
It was of Gaia combing a Lovelock
Into her long green hair.

Soon the stoker had adapted our boilers.
The new fuel? Sustainable cash
To a furnace-forge where Wittgenstein
Was reduced to smouldering Ash.

"Ahoy!" from the crow's nest. It was Capra.
"There's a strange bird winging our wake.
It's an albatross, no it's a shelduck…
No it isn't, it's a Shell-drake."

This Mayday prompted a bubbling sound
Like pots on the front of the stove
The poets had begun to uncork themselves
In their menstrual blood-Red grove.

The first weaver of words wore a black belt,
His head shaved with a razor-sharp cuttle
Not even the Penny that Ulysses loved
Had the thread of his magic Shuttle.

The storm unleashed a formidable Raine,
The forest trembled right down to the seed
In fact every tree might have washed away
But for guidance from the fluent Reed.

Those few who survived in the keepered grove
Soon began to sharpen their axes
Until it came to the ultimate chop:
Then the hatchet was Fairfax's.

This was, I'm afraid, a boozey rout,
Bottles constantly on the go,
But they'd all sign the pledge for a single malt
At the George in Hamnivoe.

Much bullion was needed to prime their pump,
Since their cash was never-ready:
Minted by dint of a non-stop spell
From our ecological Goldsmith, Eddie.

But lucky for them if they overindulged
And became incoherent and blotto
They could always infuse a purgative leaf
On instruction from Doctor Latto.

What's this? Our new merman figurehead?
Mighty ears and golden scales!
No one spoke for a moment…and then:
"Good Lord, it's the Prince of Wales!"

The bouncers have grabbed him by the scruff.
"On the fiddle! Who let you in?"
"That's alright boys, you can put him down:
It's Yehudi Menuhin."

For Traffic Warden? Obviously Porritt
Because his bite is bad as his barkin'.
He'd cry, "Do away with the motor-car,
But I reserve this space for Parkin."

Soon you could study ways and Means
On the Plains Deck in a sweat-lodge,
Or imbibe the Tibetan Book of the Dead
In a yurt with Helena N. Hodge.

You could build a sacred pleasure dome
With geomantic Critchlow,
Or plant getting on for a million trees
With the treeman Jean Giono.

We know, when it comes to planting gardens,
God tends to move in odd ways,
So how inspired of Him - or Her
To leave teaching to the Rodways.

As the days thus passed in advancement
The crew became cosmopolitan,
Until we came down to walk-about Cowan,
And the permacultural Mollison.

We'd take a bath with Michel Odent
If we felt it time to have a baby;
Or if we thought, "No wonder!"
We could check with Primavesi.

We might encounter on the afterdeck
Engaged in playing poka,
The designer Victor Papanek
With Masanobu Fukuoka.

So it's twenty-five years, and all at sea
Beats the hell out of me how we've survived.
Still I suppose if you've no destination
You've always already arrived.

That's it then, *Resurgence*.
Have this one on the house.
The work of our criminal rhymer:
I expose him - Didymus.

Issue 148 - September/October 1991

EXPERTS

WHEN I WAS eleven yet another tiresome person in a hat came all the way down to my height and said, "And what are you going to be when you grow up?" I'd had enough of this. Growing up wasn't, still isn't, on my agenda. I squinted at her in a career-orientated way and said, "A hypnotist". She batted an eyelid, which is the sure sign of someone falling into a deep trance, and staggered off in search of a plate of stuffed olives.

I recognise that over the years I've not been able to cling to that sort of power. But I'm now in a position to replace the shortfall with real conviction. I've decided that when I grow up I'm going to become an expert.

I don't mean just your everyday unpaid expert. Anyone can run to that. All you do is find some pathetic character with his head under the bonnet of his car. You say, "It's probably the alternator, have you tried tightening that one?" And when he does, and the head of the nut shears, you say how sorry you are you can't stop to sort out the problem because you have an appointment with the manager, and that personally you think anyone who isn't a member of the AA Homestart Service a perfect idiot.

Actually I'm not sure about *everyone*. For instance I suspect women aren't Grade A expert material. Take this Penelope who shares this patch with me. Reading her *pensées* I have the impression of a person who can spend the entire day looking for her lost knitting-needle and find it at bedtime when she looks in the mirror and sees she's used it to pin up her hair-bun. She'd get my nomination for Chair-person of the Inter-Galactic Vagues, but I don't think you'll catch her laying down which is the live terminal to some poor duffer with his life in his hands who's trying to change a 13 amp fuse with a carving knife. You see, you don't get to be an expert by running around in monthly cycles. What you need is a solid linear overview, and absolutely no *pensées* whatsoever.

I can think of two types of expert that I shall try to avoid becoming. The first is that currently referred to as "the expert in Brussels." This is your fulltime, career expert. Career experts, as the name suggests, are fully dedicated to being experts, which means they cannot possibly have expertise in anything other than being an expert. They can't possibly know anything about anything else, and it's part of their professional integrity to demonstrate this at every available opportunity. This means that they can be absolutely relied on to get everything wrong. Politicians are probably less reliable in this regard, which is presumably why they place such a premium on the reliability of their experts.

Whenever you read of something that beggars not only the imagination but also half the planet (like this recent disclosure that Britain currently receives in interest on loans to the Third World three times what it contributes in foreign aid), you can bet there's an expert in Brussels at the back of it somewhere.

The other expert I'm working not to become is one from what I term the Sectarian Class. Unlike the former these have stumbled on a little learning which, as we've all been taught, is a dangerous thing. This sort of expert is so turned on by the excitement of knowing something that he up and struts it about as the universal yardstick for everything from the EEC Directive on Duck Egg Production to the Doctrine of the Immaculate Conception (come to think of it that's not a very good example because these two are, at least according to *Resurgence* sectarianism, virtually synonymous). Everything in existence is reduced to the microscopic context of the sectarian expert's sectarian knowledge. You see a lot of this sort of expert in politics; wielding a sectarian know-how in something called The System. You see him being what's called *promoted* from one ministry to another so that he can impose his one system on such different things as Agriculture, Transport, Education, and Industrial Development. Also most religious experts fit into this category. They undergo training on very much the same lines as the elite SAS. This enables them to reduce everything, including God, to their own little closet of learning; which is demonstrably a *very* dangerous thing.

No, I'm looking to become an expert of a very different water: a freelance, free-thinking, free-wheeling expert who comes into the studio, says his say, grabs his cheque and gets the hell back to his own place before the teeth of his expertise begin to bite. Like the one I heard on the radio the other morning. I think he'd been drawn from some Directory of Experts, sub-title Fiscal and Economic, to comment on the double-dip recession (I don't know about you, but when I first heard that phrase I thought they were announcing a slump in ice-cream sales). He said that inflation around 5% was dandy provided it was matched by 5% growth. It took my breath away. Poor old Douthwaite (see *The Growth Illusion*), he'll be wondering what's hit him. You get it, do you? 1,000% inflation, no sweat - provided you have 1,000% growth. Now that's what I call expertise.

You don't need a think-tank to work out this sort of stuff; a real expert can come up with it in his bath.

Issue 152 - May/June 1992

SPORTING GREEN

Aabout to blow the starting whistle when my teeth began
to grind and I remembered that I can't afford to be revolting just
now. June, July...the countdown to one of the Green Calendar's
most important fixtures. The local Flower Show, and I'm in
strictest training.

In truth I've been thinking for some time that the Flower
Show might be a way of bringing sport into the green arena (or

greens into the sports arena). But as the date approaches I'm bound to acknowledge that whatever flower shows offer in terms of naked animosity and needlemanship, they fall short (and I speak here with authority) on the true sporting elixir that can transmute the most beastly human aggression into the sort of post-combat *agape* one tends to experience at the end of a bruising twelve-round title fight.

What happens at the Flower Show is not forgiven, and it's certainly never forgotten.

Certainly nobody round here seems to have forgotten the year I walked away with second prize in the runner-bean class with five of an organic variety I'd selected from a neighbour's garden. I was exposed by another so-called neighbour, one of those who spends his time checking that the grass in my garden isn't greener. He'd noticed that my runners weren't yet in flower. This nit-picking is typical of the mean-mindedness that a flower show will tap. As I pointed out at the time, we real gardeners know that growing things is just a matter of luck and muck.

The skilful part is choosing the exhibits likely to put the blinkers on a board of bent judges. If my neighbour felt so strongly about his beans, why didn't he enter them himself? He probably did. Probably he just lacked the polish that dazzles the judges.

The judges are bent, are they? Well, of course. Most exhibitors acknowledge this. You only have to read their expression when they're comparing their plate of King Edwards with the winner's. "Warty old things - just that he's sanded them down and given them a coat of T-cut."

I've had a realistic view of judges ever since the year of my supreme confidence in the beetroot division. Well-founded, because it had been a diabolical year for beetroot, and I was the only entrant. Under such conditions no judge, unless he'd been tampered with, would have hesitated. These did. Then in cold blood they cut my best exhibit in half (did they care that they were destroying precisely a quarter of my entire crop?) and pronounced the heart of it "wooden". So what? Maybe I like my beetroot wooden. Nobody else in the county could come up with any sort of beetroot - not even in fibre-glass (hey, now that's not a bad idea!). They awarded me - you're not going to believe this - third prize.

To some growers that would have been a dose of tumbleweed. But not to me - I banked the experience, and came back next year to steal the silver cup. The best vegetables in the district. As a matter of fact they weren't bad, except the parsnips - and that's where the experience paid. My parsnips were so small a *nouveau cuisine* chef in a health hydro would have sniffed at them. In a moment of realism I entered them for "The Smallest Vegetable in the Show" class but reluctantly because, while this affords the winner a certain prestige, it doesn't earn points for the cup. But when I got to the hall I saw that no one else had parsnips either: no entries. I remembered my beetroot and moved decisively. I switched to the main class. That's how life's big rewards are won - not so much your dried blood and hoof, sweat and tears, but knowing the system. The predictable judges awarded a third, which carried one point toward the cup, which was precisely my margin of victory.

Winning, I find, doesn't make one popular. My wife, as well as the friends I once had, say that I may be a bad loser but when I win I'm unbearable. Maybe, but I still maintain that the most important thing about sport is being able to turn defeat to profit. The nearest I've come to this was the year I came second of two in the "An Arrangement of Annual Flowers" class. I *always* win this class, I thought even the judges knew that. Their excuse? They said they'd found a daisy, a *perennial* daisy, in my selection. I remonstrated. I pointed out that with the slug problem in my garden not even a monkey-puzzle tree has a life expectancy of more than a year. But there was no shifting them. With what I thought was considerable dignity I picked up my entry and stormed out. Well, I thought it important that the judges saw how I felt. Straight home, straight to my workroom and, in the sort of creative rage William Blake would have approved, made a painting. It's called Second Prize. People say it carries a load of conviction. I turned defeat to profit? Not yet, but one day some idiot might buy it. Or wait…I know, I'll enter it in the 'Handicraft' class in this year's Flower Show. I'll change the title. I'll call it, 'Spot the Daisy'.

Issue 154 - September/October 1992

JUST A FEW QUESTIONS

EARLY RETURNS OF the Didymus general evaluation form have come up with some surprising results: seventy-five per cent of female phone-interviewers are called Tracey.

"Hello, this is British Telecom, Tracey speaking. In the last twenty-four hours you have reported a fault on your line."

"Yes. Thank you. Actually…" I'm trying to tell her that as things turned out the fault was not so much with the line as with me. You see, by a small oversight, I'd neglected to… But these Traceys don't want excuses, they would like you to answer a few questions.

"When you reported the fault, were you answered in (a) one minute, (b) two minutes, (c) upward of five minutes?"

"Oh, absolutely straight away. But you see there wasn't actually…"

"When the engineer called, did he locate the fault in (a) one minute, (b) in up to one hour, (c) within the foreseeable future?"

After this had been going on for (c) upward of ten minutes, I threw the phone on the floor, broke the receiver and had to go over to borrow my neighbours phone to report the fault. Poor devil, he's probably this moment answering a few questions while trying to get it into Tracey's skull that no matter what she accuses him of, it's no fault of his.

"Were you (a) entirely satisfied, (b) partially satisfied, (c) …"

"No, Tracey, nor (d), nor (e), but (f)… and you can tell Brit Telecom what they can do with it."

"How old are you?"

"I beg your pardon!"

"What is your income per annum? Above £50,000?"

This, you no doubt recognise, is from the *Resurgence* Questionnaire. And "when we have analysed all the answers and opinions, we hope to publish the results." Oh goody! But is that wise?

"Do you *adhere* to any religious tradition?"

"Do I *adhere*…mmm? Not if I can help it."

"Do you ever read through the advertising section?"

"Read *through*? He must mean see through."

You know, I've read *through* the entire questionnaire and the outstanding question of the *Resurgence* Sports Page doesn't get a mention. The kindest thing I can say is that maybe he thought this *was* a sports page. Bags of competition. "Which of the following types of books do you read most often?" I could have told him not to waste a box on fiction. And if you think that's sour grapes, why not send me a suggestion of what *you* would do with the 2000 remaindered copies of your novel that *Resurgence* reviewed with such rave. On second thoughts, don't send a suggestion, just send a carrier.

Ah, here's a good one. "Which one daily paper do you read most frequently?" The *Guardian* of course. "Of the 750 people who answered our questionnaire, 747 were *Guardian* readers." So what does that tell us? That tells us that *Guardian* readers answer questionnaires. As if we hadn't suspected it all along!

Interesting! Did you notice No. 16 is the only question that isn't a question? No question mark. Just the bald statement: Sex. And then a square box called Male, and (well I suppose you'd expect such equal opportunities in *Resurgence*) a square box called Female. You know, there's something '*Guardian*' about that square box *and* the lack of a question mark - something gloatingly self-assertive. I mean... no, on second thoughts perhaps I don't. Well, I do as a matter of fact, but I've decided to keep it to myself.

Now, wait a minute! Have you read No. 5? "My favourite sections of the magazine are: (please put in order of preference)..." Oh dear, how un-holistic! How ungreen! "The organs of my body in order of preference are..." "I like flowers better than stalks, and as for roots - yuk!" Okay, let's see what he puts first on the list. "Intellectually demanding articles". How embarrassing! You see the whole thing's loaded towards the *Guardian* reader. Personally I shall be taking legal advice. Didymus is placed eighth on the list - below even the poetry page, *even* below Business Diary. I might have been prepared to overlook that, but not the inference that Didymus doesn't qualify among the intellectually demanding articles. Just because I can perceive the attractions of a *Resurgence* Sports Page, I think he sees me as the alternative man's Vinny Jones.

Besides, the whole concept is about as scientific as an opinion poll. Take Penelope and these Pensées of hers. Her fans won't have answered for the obvious reason that they've all just melted their ballpoints trying to fish whatever it was that was burning out of the electric toaster. Then there's the Poetry Page - no one in her right mind would ever admit to reading that, and if she *did*, and if any self-respecting poet got hold of the news, he'd die of embarrassment. And what about poor old Kinsman? Year after thankless year he's been trying to coax a grain of profitability out of what must have been a pretty barren green patch... and now, along with Up the Elephant, he's dismissed as intellectually undemanding.

The truth is that if you ask a *Guardian* reader, or just about anyone else for that matter, whether they're enjoying themselves, it makes them feel uncomfortable. I think they feel that if they can't come up quickly with some intellectually demanding criticism, they may find themselves next day surreptitiously buying a copy of *The Times*. Anyway, your Didymus reader wouldn't sink to answering a questionnaire. But I'm not guaranteeing there won't be a busload with pick-axe handles outside the Editor's office if he starts announcing that the end of the season Didymus is relegated.

Issue 162 - January/February 1994

PROGRESS – A BACKWARD GLANCE

MAD. THAT'S THE name I've come up with. MAD is a degenerative phobia associated with an entirely rational fear of progress. MAD is prevalent among people not very good with buttons, and among the manually (by which I mean instruction-manually) challenged. MAD, or Mode Awareness Deficiency. The onset usually occurs when one's just given up on another Japanese instruction manual. It's then one suddenly realises that this house one had always thought so solid that, if there were a power-cut, one could grope one's way to the medicine chest…that it's nothing of the sort. It's a flimsy shell to a moaning vacuum of inter-galactic cyberspace – whatever the hell that is. I'll tell you what it is: it's the yawning capacity for this incalculable number of current in-house modes all operational at the touch of a button. Or would be if you could get your mind round the instruction manual.

To be honest, I never had much of a finger for buttons. Recently I updated my typewriter, a 1947 Hermes, a solid machine built on similar lines to Rommel's staff car. It responds

21stC for Mate

QUEEN ELIZABETH 2

operon
okay here is my first fragile tap into this century.
so far it has taken me a mere three days to get this on too
the screen. dolt yet y know how to put in caps or how the hell
tohave it printed out – and tippex doesnt work on the surface
of this screen.   nn
    with a tome the size of a long russian novel   onpn my knee i
am
trying to figure this baby into some sort of sense. as you
can tell i aint   yey got the hang on the correction buttons
there you go. now ill try to motivate the printer
the keyboard is feather sensitive......
god help me i cant get this stuff to print   – back to
instruction manual.
  unmb rgeyyth 6ll d ty l

Back to pen!

to my touch, in fact so enthusiastically that when I'm on song the 'o's fly round my head like confetti. But even this machine has a couple of buttons "that keep their secret still". That's fine by me. And one reason it's fine is that no one's trying to tell me my Hermes has a memory.

I've got this CD player. It may have a mind of its own, but by and large it does the business. And it has a number of buttons I prefer not to touch. The other day, we had staying one of those big-earning scruffy young boffins who in my day and at my school would have been scorer to the 2nd XI and rated unemployable. He said my CD player had a memory and he'd show me how to work it. He did, just as he was leaving. I admit I was excited. I had him run the process past me a couple of times, and then hurried him out of the house and waved him off - after all, there's nothing electronic about my memory. Back I dashed. Well, he hadn't been able to programme me. Though you can't always tell with boffins - he'd probably deliberately left something out. That's it, he probably wrote instruction manuals in his spare time.

Then we have this fax machine. I know, I know - but if my position as Sports Editor is ever confirmed, how else am I to get the late scores through to HQ? Buttons! It's got more buttons than a guardsman's mess-kit. And a manual in four languages. And, somewhere inside, a device which every time I touch a button goes off like an electronic cuckoo clock. I tell you, more than once that machine has had me groping for the medicine chest. Know what it's got? It's got a button called ALARM which you're invited to press if you feel out of your depth. I press it quite often, and every time the machine groans into gear and out stutters this *Reader's Digest* version of...of the Instruction Manual.

I think it might be helpful if at this point I illustrated my position with reference to *Resurgence's* late Poetry Editor, John Fairfax.

This is the man whom NASA elected to phone (he was in the bath at the time) and have him, shivering and naked, declaim to the astronauts in orbit and the attendant heavens his poem, 'Oration for a Space Shot'. The man who invented the Inflatable Mooney's Bar & Pleasure Palace, able to be deployed at short notice in potential trouble-spots, and which I'm proud to acknowledge had its first successful trial in this column. The man who was named the 1986 Vague of the Year for planting outside his window, in the earnest belief they were variegated wild flowers, the bath salts his Aunt had given him for Christmas. A man whose single-incarnation achievements range from being crowned in Korea for his prosody to being appointed Poet in the Fo'c'sle Bar for a cruise of Senior Citizens on the QE2. Unlike some of us he's a proponent of *all* forms of progress - and to prove it I've a shed out the back with a thirty-year heap of useless gadgets he's had me invest in.

In short, he's not a man to cold-shoulder the word-processor. Not even if it's state-of-the-art, rescued from his neighbour's skip, and just needs a hose-down and a good blast of WD40. Few things will ever have moved you more than the communication (illustrated above) I received from him recently. Now if it had been *that* they'd chosen to shoot into outer space to be picked up by some alien intelligence...I can't imagine a better or more heroic brief for Humankind, or for little lost planet Earth.

Issue 182 - May/June 1997

ANOTHER FINE LETTUCE

IT'S IN MID-SUMMER I feel most like the emperor Diocletian - that moment when the Editor's office is on the blower clamouring for reassurance that I've not forgotten the deadline. "My friend," I want to say, which is what Diocletian said when they begged him to return to power, "if you could see what fine lettuces I am growing, you would not urge me so hard to take up that burden again."

But what stings me to print this time is a reader's response to my recent analysis of the Electronic Revolution. And incidentally the weight of that piece, as well as my credibility, was unbalanced by the most unfortunate misprint. The printed text stated that the word-processor lifted from a neighbour's skip by the erstwhile *Resurgence* Poetry Editor, John Fairfax, was "state of the art". What I wrote, matching the words carefully to Fairfax's grasp of the Vague, the recyclable and the intermediate, was "state of the Ark". So, for a start, I'd like that corrected. Anyway, this reader suggested that, on the evidence of that piece, the long-awaited Didymus Solution to the Problem of the Motor-car was unlikely to go further than a recommendation of traffic-calming for chariot races. How wrong can a person be? I'll show you.

1) The conversion of the National Grid and the telegraph network into the Advance Transport System. Each household to be issued with a 'bubble' - an advanced concept of marrying the ski-lift to the space-capsule. Two-seater or Family Size, these suspended spheres simply clip onto the existing wires. In some areas wires may have to be upgraded to provide the necessary energy drive, and countrywide there are a few poles that may not meet the req-

uisite stress standard. A considerable outlay in fact, roughly equivalent to repainting the white lines on 330 metres of the M25 (though significantly less if you take account of the upward of two million work hours lost in resulting peak-traffic contra-flow confusion).

Each 'bubble' to be equipped with a small computer which, if you can decipher the manual, can be programmed to have you pass without any serious environmental depredation from junction box to junction box to your pre-chosen destination. Current motorway traffic will be kept off the country wires and confined to the central multi-lane pylon-system with its slow and fast tracks.

Not only will the beauty of the landscape be greatly enhanced by the perpetual motion of silently moving brightly-coloured 'bubbles', but the perhaps most noxious of current pollutants will be stemmed at source, namely the fellow-passenger with the mobile phone. Since he or she will be, so to speak, *on* the line, it's fair to assume her number will be constantly engaged.

2) Naturally the Inner City will command a very different approach. Intensive research, in fact more than one visit to our local Market Town, has established that during transition cars may be retained only by those living in excess of 14.7 miles from the nearest Superstore...but even these cars, unless involved in serious research, will not be admitted to the town centre.

The answer: covered conveyor pavements like, but well in advance of, those on-the-level escalators in fashionable airports where one gets stuck behind the chap with the unmistakable terrorist tendency, and who can't cope with his hand-luggage - while on either side the lithe lines of back-packers amble past and beat one to Immigration. No, the ones we're working on are multi-track/multi-speed pavements - you step from one speed to another at will. Outlay? Modest. Or at least modest when you take into account the savings councils will be making on traffic-war-dens and lollipop-persons. And the power-source? Now here is perhaps the opportunity for the Right Livelihood Award Committee to rectify their glaring oversight in regard to the Didymus *Two-Flannel Buff.*

City streets are without exception under-ridden by mainstream sewers...the entire mobile pavement network can thus be powered by contiguous methane converters (patent applied for), and this means that variations in off-peak demand can be governed by a single bureaucrat with powers to impose flavour-of-the-month bargain offers in all local supermarkets. In a word, to a greater or lesser extent, beans.

Right, I think now without apology I may return to my lettuces.

Issue 184 - September/October 1997

NEXT TIME ROUND

YOU'D BE BADLY shaken if I were to disclose how many *Resurgence* readers have managed over the years to negotiate me into a tight corner and, their faces luminous with ardour, confide that given choice they'd elect to be reincarnated as one of Antoinette's chickens.

Antoinette is my wife - but even so I think these people are being unrealistic if they think I'm able to exercise much influence. Nonetheless I am flattered - because these are bright punters who must have realised I'd be part of the package, and that if they're going to start crowing at four in the morning, then no matter what sort of merit they've chalked up in a former life it'll be me they have to answer to.

It's perfectly true, Antoinette does spoil her chickens rotten. But not exclusively her chickens - in fact if you're a *sentient being* in this locality (cow, dog, cat, rabbit, raven, magpie, squirrel, rat, humble-bee, woodlouse...), you'll stand a fair chance of being spoilt rotten. But before you complete your application there is something I think you should know - you stand almost no chance of getting on the list unless you're prepared to come trailing some distinctive karmic blemish. Equal opportunities are one thing, but (and this could be part of my karmic stew) we're not running a house for straightforward animals. To save you being hurt in the selection process maybe I should list the qualities of some of our most successful former candidates.

No straightforward dogs. Retrievers seem to be favoured provided they are completely off their trolleys. They all are adept at conjuring thunderstorms out of a summer sky, for the duration of which it is required they be cuddled in a darkened linen cupboard and kept out of their minds on low-potency *arnica*. This experience seems to do permanent damage to their nerves so that they emerge from the cupboard prey to obsession. One we called The Muggus (an affectionate but accurate revision of the title Magus) identified a hole in an oak tree and devoted the remainder of her non-dinner hours to standing before it in quivering apprehension that whoever wasn't in there might suddenly appear.

A cat off its trolley is even less straightforward. There was Crackle, a diminutive and dainty dairymaid with an opinion of herself so slanted that she would chase the bullocks. Or Masher, a brutal-looking tabby tom unnerved by everything, including being left on his own, so that he would follow us on walks howling, "Wait for me…Wait for me…" He left a vacancy immediately filled by Ghum. Ghum was named after a well-integrated young man from Nepal, but not even this could disguise that what secured Ghum a place in our household was repeated incarnations of specialised abnormality. As a kitten she took refuge in a tree to escape an Airedale named Chaos. When we finally persuaded her down she'd perfected her loathing for everything, and most of all for being on the ground. She doesn't even like being spoilt, and the only concession that Antoinette has ever won from her is to eat tiny helpings of fiendishly expensive food, provided it's not something she's ever agreed to eat before. Oh, and one other condition, that the food should only be offered within six inches of the ceiling, which requires her being fed on top of the welsh dresser.

And Charlie? Charlie's a neat little pink female cat with a big appetite. Antoinette says that Charlie's liver requires that she be "fed on demand". And boy, can she demand. She's also adept at swallowing her vitamin pills - that's twelve a day, the expensive ones, the blue, the yellow and the green. The pills put an edge on Charlie's hunger, blunted only by the immediate despatch and ingestion of rabbits. Charlie's lethal with rabbits. Between you and me it's a pity she's wasn't around with Lupin.

Lupin was a monstrous lop-ear with an identity problem. She lived in the hen-run and thought she might be a chicken. That is until she came in the house. Then she thought she might be a cat, and would try the idea out by mounting Masher when he was eating his dinner. Lupin had an evil temper and razor-wire on her paws, and would slash the wrists of anyone who tried to pick her up - except of course Antoinette. Antoinette adored Lupin. She called her "My video rabbit" and, when watching videos, would cuddle her on the sofa. As luck would have it, Lupin one day encountered a fox. Antoinette believes she approached the fox in good faith and suggested she might be a chicken. Either way the fox wasn't fooled.

Lupin was replaced by an underdeveloped lop-ear called Basil. Not that his ears were underdeveloped. When he played *mad rabbit* around the hen-run he looked like a locust with an eating disorder. I don't think Charlie would have touched him. Once when Antoinette was away I was left to look after him. I went to meet Antoinette at the station and the first thing she said was, "How's Basil?" I shifted from one foot to the other and said, "You know, love, I don't think Basil was a very well rabbit." That's an expression I detest, which is why in Basil's case it was appropriate. "He was perfectly well when I left," Antoinette said.

And I'm afraid - not even the chickens. There was a rooster with the deceptively benign name, Cocky-locky. His temper made one think Lupin could have been the reincarnated Florence Nightingale. He attacked everything that moved. Antoinette tried to defend him by saying that this was his nature. Which didn't cut much ice with the rest of us. At the time, our son was about four. One day Antoinette found Ben on his back with Cocky-locky perched on his chest wondering which eye to peck out first. After that she licensed me to invent something called the Hitti-cock Stick. For months none of us would venture outdoors without it. Though Antoinette was uncompromising about it being used only in self-defence.

Issue 188 - May/June 1998

SWALLOWED

I HAVE THE lamentable feeling - that they're gone.

This early morning's sharp easterly has the sky an opaque gleam, more silver than blue. Loaded, a mind looking for trouble. The gusts come fitful through the trees in bits, or bundles, sometimes a broken bale. The crinkled leaves are on edge, rustle like wrapping-paper - or, when the wind dies, I hear their intermittent foil-fall in the woods. Share-certificates falling on the dealing-room floor. Ssh, ssh, ssh!

Yesterday evening, and I'm talking here of the 4th October, the sun was out of the valley by six. So then the blue above is a world apart, and that's where and when they came, maybe forty swallows. For a time and, I like to think, my benefit they stayed, there in the blue leavings of Summer; dipping their wings a last time, a last quick-threaded embroidery cross-stitched in our patch of sky. It seemed to me though they were saving something, were perhaps a little preoccupied - that their mind (mine too if I weren't very careful) was already elsewhere.

I waved and shouted, told them I wanted them back safe, ordered close formation over the sea, a night-flight through trigger-happy Italy, told them I favoured the Nile-route, the Pyramids and Sphinx, dip for a quick one, better than a dry run on the old Timbuctoo line. Better than…but Oh, above all, that I wanted them back.

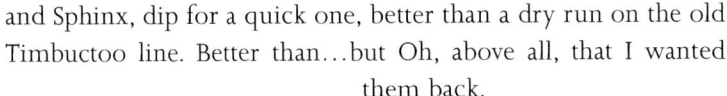

It was last year, after thirty-six vacant summers, that two swallows were persuaded to take the lease on our stable. We'd had a few prospective tenants over the years but for some reason the amenities had failed to impress. Then one year a dysfunctional couple who I guess were enjoying something of an on-off relationship and shouldn't have been considering a family set up a late rickety nest in the porch, employing the blade of my suspended machete as main-beam. A disaster - the pair of them were more interested in buzzing the cats than feeding their young. Then on a whim they were up and off to Africa leaving three dysfunctional unfledged babies for us to feed. Antoinette tried teaching them to fly. But being of the 'Example is better than Precept' school of education her efforts, frankly, were neither convincing nor a success.

But the two that came last year were a better class of bird altogether. They knew what they were after. True, they deliberated for a couple of nerve-tingling weeks, disappearing presumably to check out other possible sites. But finally vision triumphed and they settled for a sort of economical barn-conversion - a spot where adjacent wall, joist and rafter came together and, for a workable nest, required the addition of just the one external wall.

Very much a two-parent family, and well-organised to ensure minimum disruption to their lifestyle. Or to, what I take to be, their pre-eminent role in the balance of the cosmos - namely, the summer-long sleight of wing over our garden causing the eye not only to dance but to perceive how the infinities of all space can be distilled to one fleet free-fall gasp of delight. Or something...I'm not a swallow, it's the best I can do.

And soon they were joined by their kids. And mid-August by a second brood - so that suddenly our garden's allotment of sky seemed superscribed not by just two, but a whole posse and dazzle of swallows.

Winter...without swallows...on and on until...April. I was writing by the window overlooking the stable. I'd love to know what it said, that little shriek. I glanced up - four, headlong and head-to-tail, in through the stable window. They'd come back, the travellers, shadowed by the vision of all that had passed them by. Because that, in the absolute moment of their arrival, was how it seemed - the great rivers, the curve of the blue stratosphere, the smell of a continent burning, the thunder and drumbeat of names like Ngorongoro, all in proper ignorance beside the reality of the expectant nest.

The point being that it may have passed them by - but not me. The flash of their arrival, with its scintilla-impression of all they'd seen, had opened my eyes. I'd had it delivered, a kind of instant video of their journey. They might have no use for it, but to me…I felt how I had been amplified by the achievement of this world-view-come-home. And at the same time socially elevated as if Ranulph Whatshisname Fiennes had chosen out of all the orchards of England to bivouac under my apple-tree.

So there it is. We can do business, the swallows and I. Through the dreary fireside winter I'll be their janitor, keep an eye on the nest. While they do my essential travelling. This way I can remain upsides with all my peripatetic friends. By means of my swallows' first-hand agency I'll skim the snow-summit of Kilimanjaro, and plummet the roar and lion-tawny (hey, I'm enjoying this already) torrents of Kariba. I'll…I'll…

No wonder I was out there last evening, waving and shouting, "My swallows!" And all the ducks joined in, thought I was talking to them. As if! What, with their limited horizons?…they still think if they venture through the gate they'll slip off the edge of the world.

So you see it suits me. I no longer have time to travel myself. After thirty-seven years in the valley I've realised that if I'm ever to be here for as little as just one whole day I must get on with it. I need to practise. No time to swan or swallow about. I need to get nowhere…fast!

Issue 192 - January/February 1999

SCREEN TEST

Perhaps you didn't know that the *Resurgence* office has become some sort of variant of Silicone Valley. In the best tradition of investigative journalism I happened on the scandal by chance. I phoned in to ask for an address and was told with, it must be said, all the engaging transparency we subscribers so value, that the address was currently orbiting, lost somewhere in darkest outer cyberspace - *along with half the* Resurgence *database*. "Oh", I said, and I think that expressed my feelings pretty accurately. You see, last time I took a sounding the entire *Resurgence* archive, all relevant information, every detail of intelligence about the private lives of both contributors and subscribers, was loaded either in one appropriate-scale biodegradable cereal carton beside the editor's desk. Or else retrievable at the touch of a button in that unlimited inner-space - the Editor's memory.

Progress, that's what it is. And I'm very much against it. What I'm all for is the glitch, the virus and the breakdown. When I hear of another novelist who's pressed the wrong button and lost the entire draft, I'm beside myself. Or you get through to the bank or the airline: "Could you ring back, we're having a spot of bother with our computers." That's what I love. Or the Arts Centre - It's just gone blank on the booking details for the next three months. Tremendous stuff, in fact probably a progressive form of concept art. And then there's the life-leached emptiness in the eyes of those who've stared overlong into the unresponsive screen. I treasure it - for me it sums it all up. This progress that saves us all so much time and labour and leaves everyone overworked, utterly exhausted, unable to communicate, let alone answer a letter. And so in stress that they leap out at the next red traffic-light determined to rediscover the reliable old-fashioned manual method of bashing some other driver over the head.

In my view it is those screens we should hold accountable.

When our two children were finding their first small feet we quickly adopted our neighbours as grandparents - Grannie and Granfer Beer. Brilliant. You should try it. Every afternoon the children run across the lane to tea with Grannie Beer while you take a breather, put your feet up and watch... Well no, we couldn't and that's the point. No reception in the valley, so no telly. No screen. Instead we took a breather; Grannie and Granfer learned to live for their grandchildren, and our children learned their essential life-skills: how to make tiddy-pasty, how before milking to wipe the cow's titties, and how, with wine-gum lips, chocolate chin and cheeks bulging like a hamster's, to tell your Mum that no, Grannie Beer hasn't been giving you sweets. Day to day, and all the time for the children it was unfolding - the seventy years of Grannie Beer's world, a living history that touched on the valley so that the bridge and the trees and sometimes the individual stones were coloured with a wholehearted meaning no schoolbook could ever supplant.

The change seemed to happen over night. It was Auntie, one of Grannie Beer's sisters, I think, six miles away in the village who had the telly. Evenings, that's most evenings, when Granfer and Fred went to the Anchor for a drop, Grannie Beer started to have her drop at Auntie's - a cup of tea and a drop of the telly. Back at home Grannie Beer grew this faraway look in her eye.

Then into our valley stalked progress. Not much of a picture unless you were watching *Scott of the Antarctic*, but good enough for Grannie Beer. The children still went over to tea, but now they ate it in silence while Grannie Beer watched the box where it was set beside the Rayburn in the kitchen. She began to look like an old crosspatch, seemed to want to have the conversation over with, and now when she called Fred in to his dinner the sound was peremptory. Even watching the box she looked bad-tempered, ready to snap at the least interruption.

The children drifted away until the main current caught them and took them to school. Grannie Beer's seemed a world of lost content. Arthur was gone, Fred came and went making no noise

- and that left the box. One day Fred came and told us Mother was having trouble with that old woman again. We went over. It was that bad-tempered old woman in the mirror who wouldn't take her dinner. Antoinette (my wife) explained to Grannie Beer that the woman was bad-tempered because she didn't like the way Grannie Beer was looking at her. But Grannie Beer had taken a dislike to the woman and her mind was made up. So Fred had to hide all the mirrors - which improved things for a while. But the bad-tempered woman slipped back. Grannie Beer found her hiding in a drawer in the small chest beside her bed - a two-inch mirror out of an old handbag.

Now Fred's on his own. He can't get out as much as he used to. He watches the television vaguely - the snooker, Blind Date. It's some sort of company, but you sense he can take it or leave it.

But for Grannie Beer the screen had assumed reality. So then the little mirror became the screen - and the bleak truth it mirrored back was the fret of her own emptiness. Nothing any more for the children. A chain of songs, a link with past, the continuum of the heart...had broken. The screen's doing: I don't doubt it.

Issue 194 - May/June 1999

AS FAR AS IT GOES

THE PIECE I wrote a year ago about Antoinette (my wife) - about her chickens, reincarnation and the strict karmic qualifications required even by *Resurgence* readers aspiring to an after-life perch in her hen-house, caused a storm of interest. Antoinette's own appraisal was more objective. "It's alright," she said, closing the copy and returning it to its place on the margin of the kitchen table, "...so far as it goes." I gasped, "Brilliant!" I thought. "Doesn't that just sum everything up? I mean the Green movement. I mean *Resurgence* itself." I resolved then and there - this time I'll finish the job.

Later I learned that she had referred specifically to my account of Cock-locky, her homicidal rooster, who terrorised our community, whom she adored, and for whom I was finally licensed to invent, in purely defensive capacity, the *hitty-cock-stick*. It's true, there was more to the story, but full context required two items of background information. Scoop material they may have been - but no, as usual the Editor wasn't prepared to cede me a couple of inches of his contents page.

The first was this: Antoinette's family hail from Gubbio, a city that would be off the map if St. Francis hadn't negotiated a deal with the voracious wolf. The indicative second is that her patronymic, Galletti, means (something she concealed from me till after our marriage) a hit-squad of the most evil-tempered little fighting cocks. In this case her posse of bantam cockerels. They ganged up on Cocky-locky and in one night reduced him to the intensive care unit in the kitchen. *Arnica, hypericum*, hands-on and whichever sort of counselling it is where the client doesn't get much of a say. Yes, another miracle. He emerged pacified and what Antoinette termed "a real gentleman". In fact something of a

role-model for our son, Ben, and myself - in the way he took grain from the hand, allowed the ladies to enter first and finally earned his come-uppance in heroic confrontation with a buzzard.

"As far as it went" also omitted mention of Salome. My original point was that the corrective opportunities of Antoinette's *ménage* are not wasted on straightforward animals, but reserved for those trailing serious baggage. Some are slow to reveal this baggage. Not so Salome. In fact in my book Salome and baggage are more or less synonymous. Antoinette's house-cow - a red Devon-cross. And cross by nature, or possibly because it's unsettling to be called Salome when you're by quite some distance the ugliest cow anyone can remember ever having seen.

She arrived healthy enough, but soon the karmic miasmas began to surface. Mastitis was readily contained with *pulsatilla*. But the hump and the cowpox were intractable. Particularly in the baggage department - and this was sorely aggravated in summer by the flies. A distinguished craftswoman was staying and Antoinette bespoke from her on Salome's behalf a voluminous protective white linen bra. It was hard to tell what Salome thought of this, but she agreed to sport it in the meadows - to all the world's astonishment.

And then our daughter, that's Elsbeth, she too thought the piece had stopped short of the real business. It had failed to mention her dog, Dana. Dana, I was forced to concede did merit a mention. Even though as a dobermann she was able to protest some of the rudest good health the animal kingdom can have ever devised. Something she vigorously maintained even after a shift in Elsbeth's life had this entanglement of energy move in on us on a kind of end-of-season free transfer.

In common with everyone else Dana found Ghum, the black

cat, intolerable. Otherwise the only thing that discountenanced her was the cold. She slept under several duvets. Daily she demonstrated how there is no need to bear malice - provided you are sufficiently thick-skinned. When she stole your lunch, not even the most severe beating could distract her from enjoying it to the full. To me that seemed to suggest she'd passed beyond the toils of karma. Yes, but as if I would know.

The first sign that she might have more than a chance appointment was fetched when Antoinette, one cloudless morning alone in the house, was giving vent to *Ave Maria*. Suddenly she was in duet with a rubicund contralto…Dana. Thereafter, particularly near the full moon, the pair of them would often put their heads back and howl together. For some reason Tess, the retriever, found the performance intensely depressing, and would stand with her back to them, the vacancy of her gaze reflecting the emptiness of her dinner bowl.

Easy to suggest we should have known that even the rudest good health can mask a fatal karmic underlay. Dana's true credential finally presented itself in something beastly called Wobblers Disease. I assumed at first that this was merely to do with her unreliable *vibrato* in the C register. But no, this was more of a terminal wobble. Even so her spirits remained high and her appetite rude. And of course Antoinette was there - and so able quite near the end to support Dana in what with hindsight I realise was the triumphant closing duet from *Cavalleria Rusticana*.

Issue 196 - September/October 1999

PADDED UP

LOOK, IF YOU'RE just dropping into *Resurgence* on the off chance... if you haven't done the spadework (and that means having stuck with this column for at least twelve years), then kindly move along to the centre of the magazine where the Editor stacks the largely indigestible green products which apparently do the trick with beginners. This column is strictly for the hardcore - people in the front line looking for real solutions to real problems. For instance, moles.

In olden times moles, in my experience, were largely confined to the lawn of one-time *Resurgence* Poetry Editor John Fairfax, better known as the inventor of Murphy's Inflatable Pleasure Dome. In those days moles were jocular little creatures whose antics I, for one, found a source of innocent year-round entertainment.

As of 9th Jan 2000 all this suddenly changed. Moles declared themselves a major threat to the environment. They came tunnelling up the valley with an inevitability that makes global warming seem like a small thermostat problem with the back boiler. By the 15th a cell was engaged in subversive activity in the orchard. The next day, there before my eyes, the first earthwork was erupting on the front lawn. Or more accurately that sacred turf where currently trials are being conducted to perfect Boloki, a game so intricately rule-ridden that, once established on the international stage, it stands an outside chance of restoring pride to the British sporting public. But let's not stray from the point.

If you are a seasoned reader of this column, you'll not be expecting its author and inventor of the Two-flannel Buff to have caved in to the first mole. I diverted the stream and flooded the lawn. Not, I hasten to assure the Editor, to drown the moles; simply to deliver a stern message. This resulted in a very important discovery. Moles are thinly disguised aquatic animals in whom a quick dip induces the kind of buoyant hyperactivity more usually connected with a school of porpoises. Yes, but then how often does The Flood end with a rainbow? I refer to the solution, green in all essentials, that has eluded every gardener since Adam, and which I now pass on.

One large rectangular plastic fishtray (you'll find them delivered regularly to North Devon beaches by the autumn gales). Six stretches of wide-bore garden-hose of various lengths. The fishtray is placed upside down in the middle of the lawn, which now resembles a scale-model of some legendary London underground system whose service is sickeningly predictable. With a prod identify the main lines. And at various points insert into the labyrinth the ends of the lengths of hose, being careful that they don't get blocked with earth. Then run all the hoses back to the nerve centre or operational HQ in the fishtray. Insert new longlife batteries in your small plastic radio. Place the radio under the resonant sound-box cum amplifier which by simple visionary conversion the fishtray has now become. Switch on the radio to full blast and listen as the tannoys of all the lawn's underground stations reverberate.

And that's the end of it? Not quite. So far it's been technograsp that's led the way. But now, as so often, psychological acumen is required if we're to hit the target group. Choice of programmes. Stray onto Radio 3 and before you know it you'll be hosting something akin to the Last Night of the Proms mole-style. Radio 2 and you risk achieving of the lawn the mud-bath of a Glastonbury Festival. So what have we got left? Radio 4? I wouldn't risk it - you'd be dealing with at best a win-some lose-some programme. Surely not Radio 5? Ah, now you're talking. Twenty-four hours of news and sport.

What was I providing on this very day? Every fifteen minutes there's breathless report from Jonathan Agnew. He sounds as if he's run up all the stairs of someone's Telecom Tower. A one-day international: England versus South Africa. We all know the form. England's decline starts early, and then goes into a sharp decline. Still *we* don't have to listen... tell you what, the moles do.

By midday all signs of turbulence on the lawn have ceased.

3.30 in the afternoon and Antoinette, my wife, returns from feeding the chickens with disturbing news. Or rather with thoroughly encouraging news of frenzied disturbance in the hen-run. There's a burden of probability that it was young Agnew who did the trick. Moles evidently can't do what moles do with their diggers over their ears - rather than be landed in a blind alley with news of decline bottoming out in yet another collapse of the mid-order, those moles had dug under the three-foot foundation of a substantial garden wall, underpassed a new-laid hardcore track, and were going ballistic in the hen-run.

So there it is, free of charge and foolproof. One caveat though: if moles are as keen on the Summer Game as the rest of us, and if England did have a bit of a run against the Windies, then you'll have to move the equipment into the chicken-run quick. Or else they'll be back.

If you listen to Test Match Special, you'll know young Agnew's always bragging about living in something called the Vale of Beaver. I don't know a lot about the common or garden habits of beavers. But I can tell you with absolute certainty that if you're living in the Vale of Beaver and suffer from moles, then you're tuned to the wrong programme.

"Oh dear!" As Henry Blofeld was once heard to remark.

Issue 203 - November/December 2000

AND LEAVE THE HOUSE FREE

D**ID I MENTION** that Fred Beer has died? The year before last, at Christmas. He was eighty and had lived his life here in the valley, and was our neighbour for forty years. Firstly along with his father, Arthur (who as far as I know was all his long life over the way at Watergap) and Dolly, his mother, and later with just Dolly, and then on his own.

We have a photograph of Arthur and his brother Alfie and his little sister Lilian, taken we reckon in 1902. Just as wonderful a photograph as could ever have been. The three children so alive, and so unassumingly assured of their liveliness that it seems unalterable that they and their landscape (which is barely altered in a hundred years) are each the other's possession. The one reality…or the one figment. Looking at that photograph it strikes me that the universal magic that surrounds us all is somehow convened in that moment into a predetermined here and now. As if before that, here was where it (whatever it was) was headed, and after that moment each moment was another moment away. When I look at the photo I feel exposed - my foot in the valley seems in forty years to have left a very tenuous print. In fact I feel I should tread even our meadows with a curious delicacy because, while there's certainly nowhere else I belong, I can't be altogether confident I belong here either.

I was twenty-four the year I arrived, and I think it was the year I wrote a small poem I titled *Ages*. Four ages, eight lines: to each age a couplet. The last couplet reads:

Knows how to depart
And leave the house free

Forty years closing the gap on my dying has shown me that leaving the house free may be easier said than done. But now, as with a number of other tricky simple things, Fred has taken me to school.

Fred generally had trouble with his breathing, and towards the end it was just too much of an effort. Finally the day came when he himself couldn't manage the breathing any more, which meant something or someone else would have to take over.

Which meant the hospital - which meant leaving Watergap. Antoinette, my wife, who packed his bag and took him on his way, never doubted he'd accepted he was leaving for good. Or if not for good, simply for ever.

Some minutes after they'd gone I went from our place across the lane - I think I imagined I would somehow be with Fred. But he was gone. Watergap was empty, uninhabited. The Rayburn was still going, and there was plenty enough around to touch on memories. But Watergap has been vacated. And the next day it was the same. No sense of violence and nothing heavily stated - just the clean here and now, with nothing to impede or spook whatever the future had in store.

So had Fred not been attached? The valley wasn't just his earth, it was his everywhere. And whatever his attachment, I guess it was so unconsidered and inclusive a fact that it didn't feature in his questioning. Unless some wonderment came to him those last summer evenings I saw him leaning on the meadow gate, his cap pushed back, the old cat lounged shoulder to shoulder round the back of his neck, watching down the valley the swallows in the sunlight slaloming midge to midge over the stream.

So what were the memories...from the slow-turning years before ever I arrived? Hay-making like as not. As a boy there'd been Arthur's shire horse: the hay-making horse-power, and that same slow manpower that built the meadow banks or the two leats a mile in all to drive the mill. And much of the memory would have been the quiet: harness-shake, switch of the tail, stream and birdsong and the call to tea.

When I arrived it wasn't a lot different. Except now the stutter of the Fergie, and evenings the old Morris leaving for The Anchor, and finding its own way home gone eleven. But change was the order and was in something of a hurry. It didn't seem to hurt so much at first. The sound of the milking machine was sleepy in the summer evenings, continuous to the clink of pails and the scuff of hoof. I helped with the hay. The horse had gone and the scythe, but still it was hayforks to turn, toss and load first the wagon and then the rick with the sweet sun-scented stuff - a small enough skill but one which with the thirsty tiredness of evening made one feel part of the round and slow-breathing of the earth.

But then on the back of the tractor came the spinner that laid the hay in neat rows ready for the pickup, packing and racket of the baler. I think this was what's called labour-saving - it meant you no longer sampled the hay, and that what was once a bit of an art was reduced to a slog. You paid the baler by the bale, so Fred wasn't wasting time with small bales. Down in the damp where the grass was heavy with reed, it was all a man could do to lift a bale, knee it up to his chest and continue the lift to arm's length to the man building the load. You lifted the bales by the twine, and when they got round to binding with nylon, then for a writer's hands it was blisters by dinner, and by tea raw to the bone. Not that tea ever changed - and you'd go without fingers for a week for a bit of Mother's pasty.

Anyhow, hay's done with long since - and my better guess is that Fred's mind was settled back before that. Back to a time before silage and slurry when there were still fat trout in the stream, and never a lad not to have tickled one for his tea. The real hay is just another memory, like Fred's cows that went with the quotas. And now this spring day all the hills around are silent. The clarion of lambs was stopped abruptly last week - heaps of wool lying in the fields. What would Fred, leant on his gate, be thinking? More than likely not a lot. If it wasn't in his valley, this old virus, then it was elsewhere, and elsewhere is neighbours to nowhere at all. Sutcombe or Siberia...it's not a lot of odds.

Gone, and left the house free. Nothing of his; no behest, no bequest to hold back the future, nor to hurry it on. And now I'll tell you something, the moment forgives it all. In fact my best guess is that if it were this evening Fred was leaning on his gate, he'd not be wasting precious breath digging over the past. There'd be plenty enough to hand, and to ear and eye. The stream full and run clear, chattering after the rain. The thrush - yes, thrushes are back this year, thank God. No swallows yet, but so many birds.

New grass in the meadows, and along the path the celandine open in the sunshine like the milky way gone to butter. Gorse and blackthorn on the hill, and in the hedges already the bluebells and...and already so many flowers. Not that Fred could be doing with flowers, not if they weren't businesslike on the kidney beans. Which makes it worth telling that the day he was buried, a properly dark day in December, I stopped by on the way up to the church, to feel again if there was anything abroad in the house, half-expecting, I think, there'd be a wavering of voices from the room at the end, the glee of the famed Boxing-Day party at what was called Watergap Arms, with Fred behind the bar responsive to the room's sway, Arthur on his squeeze-box leading the carols, and Auntie Dora's laugh like she was a rooster who's laid an egg...but no, just the immaculate emptiness. So when I was leaving, but, wanting to stop a moment longer, I took a glance round the back, and there in the wreck of Dolly's flower-bed, on a winter-wrecked old bush was (I'm telling you this ridiculous truth) one red immaculate rose.

Issue 210 - January/February 2002

TWENTY-TWENTY VISION

TWO RIDDLES. Riddle one: what do the following have in common - Moses, Mao, St Paul, Saddam, Mohammed, Mugabe, Bush, Blair, Sharon and, we may as well face it, Schumacher? Give up? They're all men. Riddle two: what on earth can we do about it? Give up? I don't blame you.

Anna Bambridge tells ('Changing Vision', *Resurgence* 216) how at the age of three science certified her as short-sighted - and then prescribed the specs that would significantly implement the diagnosis. Her story is an unbeatable metaphor for the way mankind goes about his business, and is able to discount not just the relevance but even the existence of the feminine vision: the astigmatisation of woman by the regulatory imposition of male-tinted blinkers.

Anna Bambridge visits her optometrist to have him verify that her natural methods of vision therapy have been effective. She reads his letter-chart straight off, no specs. What does the optometrist say? He says, "You shouldn't be able to do that! You shouldn't be able to see that much. Why don't you put your glasses back on?" You can hear him, can't you? Edgy, but still trying to pull technological rank. He's telling her she's irrational, and so doesn't exist in a real thinking-man's world. You think I'm overstating it? Look at what Anna says about wanting to conduct research into how she came to see without glasses: "I was trying to prove that I was seeing every day with my own eyes, but there was no theoretical framework in which to conduct any research that was intelligible to my own experience. Any work that would be academically acceptable had to be built in a framework in which I was a logical impossibility."

This optometrist was simply displaying the old masculine dread of feminine power that since The Fall has had him thinking up rules, religions and particularly commandments to keep all her witchy stuff out of the picture - and at the same time keep her focussed on the one thing he'll admit she's good at, which is producing more men.

The one thing men are good at is thinking up religions. Whereas women don't seem any better at it than they are at map-reading. Someone needs only to have a mild out-of-body experience for men to be in there like a shot. Presto, a new religion? Or let us say another male-bonding club complete with articles, memoranda, commandments, line-managers and, very important, dogma. As soon as that's in place they're able to slap a patent-order on the experience and so ensure that if it does offer a short-cut to heaven then it's for members only. And women? One, they're irrational, and so don't really exist. Two, it's a man's club, so they don't meet the criteria. Three, there's no box on the entry form for them to tick. I meant to say, men are also good at criteria and forms.

Men invent religions to keep women out of the picture, and to legitimise their own strong-arm tactics. And this empowers them to set up another form of men's club: government. Religions are governed by men, and governments are governed by men. Very occasionally a woman is allowed in, but only if she admits she doesn't really exist and is prepared to prove this by observing the rules of the men's club, and behaving like a man. I won't score cheap points by mentioning Mrs Thatcher. Mrs Thatcher behaved like a man by going to war as soon as the opportunity presented itself. That's another thing men are good at: going to war and bloodying the nose of the opposition. Mrs Thatcher as she entered 10 Downing Street prayed with St Frances to be made an instrument of Peace - and then starting swinging her handbag.

Look at the world's trouble spots: Ulster; Israel, the Balkans, the USA, Afghanistan, Zimbabwe... No, save yourself: the whole world's a trouble spot and everywhere government equals men's club. It's a terminal problem. We need to do something about it. No one in their right mind would want women in charge - I mean not sole charge. What we need desperately is balance.

We hear a lot about democracy being the ticket - particularly from men's clubs who are keen to impose it on everyone by force. I was just now thinking there's something fishy about this when as if hit over the head with a live handbag I have this crowning idea. Whole Democracy: each constituency shall elect two members, one man, one woman. Now there's an economy of words to stoke the dole queues of Brussels! But suddenly I hear a whisper, "It won't work." I look round. "And why not?" I snarl, ready to use force if required. The whisperer sighs and then - talk about economy - just the two words, "Estelle Morris." I collapse. She's right. You can stack the house with women, but if it's men in charge of the order-papers...forget it.

But I remain on the case. What we need is a new seating arrangement. And the vision that is coming into focus is of the UN General Assembly being conducted on the lines of an Italian Sunday lunch. The whole family present, including children and dogs. And Grandmother in the chair.

Issue 219 - July/August 2003

THE GREEN PLANET

A **COUPLE OF** days before last year's Welcombe Horticultural Show I found young Rosser hiding in our garden, along with his mate Mick, known hereabout as the Suicidal Birdman - though my guess is that he's more accurately described as a form of serial space-cadet. I need to check this with John Fairfax, our former Poetry Editor - it's a term he uses frequently, and he is of course an authority on such things, having one of his poems currently on board a space-probe, bringing evidence of human savvy to the dim outskirts of the universe.

Anyway, young Rosser asked if I happened to know the latest Test Match score. Crafty. I could have fallen for this, but with the Show just two days away my guard was up. Might he have lifted my onion? Maybe not, but I do have my secrets which, I imagine, command bounty similar to the former whereabouts of Saddam Hussein.

Young Rosser recently celebrated his 50th birthday. But he looks young in a kind of organic well-composted way - a thing he has in common with his cauliflowers. I don't know how far the local LETS scheme extends, but it's clear to me he's into some barter deal with the Devil. Involving undated youthfulness. And what's in it for the Devil? Young Rosser's cauliflowers of course.

A word about these cauliflowers. Many of us trace our involvement with the Green Movement back to reading in the late sixties of cabbages grown in a windswept car park at a place called Findhorn situated unpromisingly not only in Scotland but way, way inside the Arctic Circle. The reported magnitude and aural field of these cabbages could herald nothing less than a New Age. And to anyone able to lay hands on the secret a realistic chance of at least getting upsides with Ernie Short at the Welcombe Horticultural Show. Devil or no, that secret has fallen to young Rosser - as evinced by cauliflowers whose size, when we can no longer avoid the subject, is reckoned in terms of acreage.

And now the disturbing bit. One day I returned from my shed to find Antoinette on the terrace, looking perplexed. "You've lost something," I said. "A cauliflower," she said. I nodded. Losing things the size of the cauliflowers I grow is both a common and a garden occurrence in our life. But then she added, "One that Mr Rosser gave me." I gasped. Then looked round, scratching my head. There'd be more chance of mislaying the Millennium Dome than one of young Rosser's cauliflowers. I felt I should be on the case right away. "When did you last see this cauliflower?" "Well," Antoinette said, "we'd made it out of the car..." "Hang on, *we?*" "Yes, the pair of us, me and the cauliflower. We'd got this far, and I was thinking how many meals it would make, when I wasn't here any more - I was down there by the stream looking for watercress. When I got back here it was gone. I've looked everywhere." There are times when it's best to keep matters light. "Probably aliens," I said. "Yes," she said, "probably." I'd started to say, "Don't be so daft!" when I felt an extra-terrestrial tingling behind my knee. So I said, "Keep calm!" "It's you who need to keep calm," she said. "I'm trying," I said.

We looked everywhere. In the bedroom, the tool-shed, the larder. We looked in the attic and the cupboard under the stairs. "Maybe you dreamt it," I said. "*Rosser's* cauliflower." She said. "Not in your *wildest* dreams." Which was hurtful. I rang young Rosser on the sly. She was right: she hadn't been dreaming. We kept looking for days. We looked downstream as far as the sea, we looked in the chicken-run and in the compost heap. First thing, I'd peep through the curtains to see if the cauliflower had returned. From space - outer, inner, you name it.

After two weeks I'd recovered sufficient nerve to again discuss Alien involvement. But Antoinette now appeared impatient with the suggestion. Not that she doubted it, just that she took it personally that these *entities* showed less interest in her than in Rosser's cauliflower. "I shouldn't read too much into it," I said. "Probably they've already got the low-down on humans. Probably what they're into now is some form of inter-planetary bio-espionage."

That started me thinking. Little green men, everyone knows where they come from - Mars. The Red Planet. We'd better keep our night vision trimmed. Someone up there is about to sweep the board at the local Horticultural Show. Then what? We all know what happens when you introduce alien vegetation. Japanese Knotweed! A week later monoculture rules: the Red Planet turns green. And young Rosser's cauliflowers have achieved their first step in the colonisation of the universe. You see, I was right: space cadet. You can tell a man by the company he keeps.

Issue 223 - *March/April* 2004

GREEN SMOKE

YES, I DO, I smoke ... a bit. Good to have got that off my chest - the fact, I mean, rather than the smoke and other related matter. I know it's a disgrace; I accept that you'll probably not wish to be associated with the magazine, and I'll do what I can to persuade the Editors to refund your subscription. But before you decide finally I guess that being an open-minded *Resurgence* reader you will wish to take account of my plea of mitigation.

I'm not like Fairfax, that old mate of mine and sometime *Resurgence* Poetry Editor. He's a *total* disgrace. He smokes fags - and fags is the brush by which all us enlightened smokers get tarred.

Fairfax has recently, in I should say the privacy of his own home, celebrated the sixty-fifth anniversary of his first serious fag. His health is fine but is, he claims, somewhat undermined by the government's insistent really noxious health warning on the packets. I can't honestly say that Fairfax is a light smoker: if you want your living room to look like a circa 1845 Black Country tap-room, you ask Fairfax to house-sit for the weekend. He'd bring his own fags. So that's the first part of my plea; I'm not like Fairfax: I eschew fags.

And I don't chew tobacco either. So I'm not like Jock, my other old mate - and that's the second part of my plea. It is possible that Jock doesn't actually chew tobacco, but he comes as close as possible to doing so. He smokes in a pipe something called Walnut Plug - almost certainly the very substance that salt-rendered mariners were able to chew to the consistency requisite for plugging a leaking hull, and probably the reason they were referred to as Jolly Jack Tar. Jock's definitely high tar. If you were looking for a readily applied autumn tar-wash treatment for your fruit trees, you could tether Jock for a couple of days somewhere central in the orchard. November's the best month. Keep him plugging away with the Walnut and once he's fully alight he'll have the business done in no time. He's that much of a disgrace. As a smoker I'm light years apart from Jock.

What I do is occasionally smoke a Havana cigar. As a *Resurgence* reader you will know that cigars are craft products; mine in addition are those favoured by Fidel himself: two points in my favour. I do also smoke a pipe. A disgrace? Not so fast - just wait till you read the label on my tobacco tin:

Pure Perque, derived from tobaccos smoked by American Indians in their pipes of peace, has been added to a base of coarse cut Virginian mixture to give a distinc-

tive flavour to this hand-blended mixture.

When, after supper; I am well lit up (selflessly, since even my tobacco carries a strenuous health warning) I breathe into the planetary ether a seemly smoke which inhaled passively by the *Resurgence* diaspora will make a significant contribution to the peace of the world. So throw the first stone if you must, but only if your personal emissions, carbon or otherwise, are nearer to zero.

And while I'm about it there's another smoking issue which in this magazine seems to have run to earth. Fox-hunting. Seasoned readers will recall that Antoinette, my wife, runs an intensive care unit for sentient beings on a sound equal-opportunities basis. Currently the ward is crowded with bumble bees on honey-drips. There was the time she cajoled her nine call-ducks to their night-time hutch - they entered with the compliance of the pure of heart. In the morning, when she went to let them out she found, cowering in the midst of their comprehensive disassemblement, a fox. He must have entered the hutch before them. Antoinette put grief on hold - the fox wasn't well: a case of mange. She rang the RSPCA and arranged for his or her painless delivery. This happened incidentally the very day I'd completed a fox-proof compound every bit as secure against terrorist attack as the US pentagon. And all this I mention because I don't want anyone thinking I harbour a sissy pro-fox perspective.

No: my perspective is more, I would call it, sectarian. Long association with *Resurgence* has left me not entirely un-persuaded by the doctrine of *karma* and the transmigration of souls. So now the only explanation for the delinquent and sanguinary behaviour of foxes that satisfies me is that they must have been huntpersons in a previous incarnation; and that the only karma that could provide accurately for the lifestyle of a huntsperson is that they come to experience as a fox what it's like to be hounded by a pack of baying huntspeople. Might the hunting ban not be upsetting some nub and revolvement upon which the balance of the cosmos is founded? I can see there's a case for bringing this karmic loop to a close - but can we really afford to let these last blooded huntspeople off the wheel? There's no knowing what they might get up to next. As you would expect, I do have a solution. They should be served by a new form of remedial porridge. By means of electronic tagging we can supervise them sitting down each evening after supper to smoke a pipe. We'll steer them away from the Walnut Plug towards my tobacco. They will then not only suffer the improvement of being viewed as a despicable minority, but at the same time will be making a substantial contribution to the peace movement.

Issue 223 - November/December 2005

GOVERNESS

WE DON'T WANT nuclear energy, but we do have pressing need of those deep-earth repositories designed to safekeep incalculably noxious material for a minimum of a hundred thousand years. Twenty centuries of research have failed to come up with anywhere else sufficiently out of the way for the secure impoundment of sacred texts.

Sacred texts? Yes, as opposed to holy texts. Holy texts are the ones like the *Song of Songs*, the poetry of Rumi, the *Rāmāyana*, *A Midsummer Night's Dream*, and the little poem by Ralph Hodgson that begins:

'Twould ring the bells of Heaven
The wildest peal for years
If Parson lost his senses
And people came to theirs...

These texts are what Ivan Illich called 'convivial tools' - they promote happiness and a universal coming together which (and we don't need Eric Fromm to point this out) is a good thing. The sacred texts that need to be put out of the way are on the other hand divisive, encourage men to behave badly, and are much more common. They all hotline from God whom they generally concur is a Bloke in the Sky who is unlikely to forgive you for anything, least of all noticing he's a dead ringer for Rupert Murdoch with a white beard. If you suppose this commonality might underwrite universal accord, you'd be wrong. Each claims to offer its subscribers 'chosen' status, advancement and unrepeatable perks both on Earth and afterwards in an upmarket form of the Club Med in the sky.

Sounds harmless, but actually it's not, because the blokes who get paged by the hotline then put on strange hats or turn their collars around and declare this or that patch the Holy Land that anyone in his right mind would die for.

Holy Land, oh boy! Some of us might think that if we cleared away the brigades of men behaving badly, the Holy Land would no longer be featured by some trumped-up-rock, or mountain or island or football stadium, but by the entirety of not our but this jewel-like planet that belongs to the universe - and I know a couple of bugs, a butterfly, a toucan and a whiting that tend to agree with me.

Oh Lebanon... I was in Lebanon in 1963. My mate and I hitched from Beirut to dreamy Byblos, and then back and up scented mountains to see the cedars. A young nun went out of her way to hand us each the fullest orange we'd ever tasted. A man giving us a lift took us to a sublime shepherd's stone cot near the snowline where we slept in a room through which tumbled an icy brook and whose window looked down over that most beautiful land to the distant sea. I remember us thinking it an enclave of civility and peace.

Next day, we hitched on into Syria. The driver who picked us up wore the smile of a *djinn*. He explained why we were certain to be killed... if the Muslims thought we were Druse or Christian, if the Syrians thought we were Jordanian, if the Sunnis thought we were Shi'as, if the Arabs thought we were Israelis, if almost anyone guessed we were English... He told us on no account to enter Damascus: people the day before were being strung up on the street... and then he ran through the list of possible causes again.

We crossed into Jordan, made our way to Arab Jerusalem and after a day or two, on to Galilee to put our feet up beside the lake. The first night we had supper in a café, and a robust, informed waiter pointed across the water to the Golan. "That's where Jesus drove the pigs into the water. But the pigs came back!" The Holy Land. Boy, oh boy!

Ah, time for negotiation - thank God for the United Nations. "Good point, Mr Bolton - we'll stop killing children from Friday." A moratorium, of course! Men behaving badly. And what about women? Isn't there anything they could do? Miss Burge would have known what to do.

When I was five there was a war on. My father did the manly

thing and got himself killed. My mother, sister and I tried to get on without him. Our circumstances were such that my mother was able to engage no less than a governess to keep us in line. Miss Burge. Miss Burge didn't believe in negotiation. I guess she knew that negotiation was merely a way of accommodating existing bad behaviour: no solution. And no substitute for "Behave yourself *at once!*" When I did something unrepeatable, Miss Burge led me by the ear to the bathroom and told me to sniff the ammonia bottle. Phew! You try it. I'm not sure that *Resurgence* approves of a detergent… I mean deterrent policy. But it works. Or it worked with me.

And my point is that there may be something special in a woman's way of handling things firmly because the very next week on the way back from feeding the chickens, I proposed to her. To be honest I think I caught her on the rebound. Anyway it never came to anything and she died a spinster. But the climate had changed. The ammonia went back on the shelf. Now, when the unrepeatable happened she would simply say in an astringent tone, "You will kindly stop doing that!" And I would stop.

So there you have it: men behaving badly require a governess. "Stop it! Would you *kindly* stop it!"

Issue 239 - November/December 2006

TIME FOR A YARN

A**PPLE TIME AND** the big winds would soon be up the valley to deal with the leaves. I was stripping the dry kidney-bean runners from the bamboo trellis. Looked round the way one unaccountably does to find Stephen standing in the track beside my patch, come to see if there was grass enough still growing for his few sheep up in the little plat. He nodded, glanced back over his shoulder vaguely, the way drinking cattle do, and nodded again. I stretched my back and said through gritted teeth, "Not so young as I was yesterday." You get to know from the set of a man when the time is right for a yarn, and the creak in one's back is as good a way to get started as any.

I remember - get on, can it be forty years? - You'd be driving the backway to Hartland, or out past Loatmead to Bradworthy through the lanes, and you would come on two cars stopped side by side, impassable, the driver windows wound down, the drivers set for a yarn. So what you did was draw up a polite way behind. After a time the driver headed your way would turn his head slowly and look at you or past you, and then turn back with some other thing he'd thought of to say. So you turned off the engine and wound down your window and the country you might altogether have missed was there to meet you: the backchat from the hedge, and beyond it the confidentialities of the sheep, this bit of breeze, the underview of the sky ... When all's well said and done the pair of them drove on. And the one as he passed you would spare a nod, and you would nod back a little shy knowing that whatever had turned up in the telling it must have been a thing complete, and you in some way had been in on it all.

These days more than likely I'd be someone in a hurry with my hand on the horn - like I'm in a jam on the Via Veneto.

Anyhow, Stephen and I were now well set. A decent yarn finds its own story. Nothing that *needs* saying can get a look-in, knows how it would be a rude interruption. We dealt with the weather, and the way the grass was growing like it was June. He eyed my beetroot and said that the wife liked a beetroot and this year they'd let her down proper. "You have your pick," I said, and then showed him what I really rated, my celeriac - and he looked at them doubtfully as if they were some sort of foreign trade. So then we turned on the world. Can't say we unearthed anything new - paperwork, bureaucracy, the ones that don't have even a clue ... oh, and regulations. *Unearthed*, that just about sums it all up. Sums them all up! Well one does have to laugh. Which has us remembering Jack Gifford and his way with regulations.

When you've come round to Jack you're back in the mainstream of all yarns. I found I was telling Stephen of how summer evenings, winding home late from the pub through the valley's blue-green shadow and passing None-go-by Cottage (traffic was different then) Janny would signal me to stop. I'd wind down my window and he'd lean forward with his elbows on the rim, take what was left of a pipe from his mouth, rid himself of a wondrous loop of brown spit, and fetch out of nowhere the memory that fitted his fancy. That moment had no choice but to relate to what he told, from somewhere back along, so much in full colour and alive that the present could only look on in envy. Shipwrecks, bees that could bite, what was said when he caught old Duncan the poet poaching his mushrooms ... And all the while the sky was inching to Indigo, and the tawnies carrying on like a Greek chorus, and me blinded by the blue star-gleam of mischief from Janny's eyes and deafened by the mage-work of his words to all but the world of his making. And how finally I'd freewheel on home down the lane feeling rich from a visit to a world realer that merely real.

When Stephen was gone and I was back untangling the kidney-bean stalks, I got to wondering why being stopped for a yarn should leave me revived, more sure of my ground - in some glimmer of a way come home. Nothing new as a boy, when the old hedger came round once a year with his stick and his billhook, doing the lane outside our place, I'd pass the time of day with him. Not that he said a lot, but when he sat for his dinner he'd break me a bit of crusty bread and pare me a slice of cheddar with his pen-knife and I remember thinking that if there was more to life than some other's ambition could take care of it.

A countryman then, born to it - same as Stephen and Jack. So maybe here's the point: what sense we make with the words we say comes from what we are. And the bulk of what we are comes from what we've lived, and how and mostly where. A man of the soil can't help himself - even when he's not saying a lot, what he says comes straight from what he does know - comes straight from the Earth. The Earth's in no hurry: proper place for a yarn.

Issue 245 - November/December 2007

www.resurgence.org.uk

Also available from Resurgence

THE BEAUTY OF CRAFT
A Resurgence Anthology
Edited by Sandy Brown and Maya Kumar Mitchell

"Resurgence has always supported the crafts. The wide-ranging essays in this splendid anthology testify to that commitment to both nature and culture." — Tanya Harrod, author of *Craft in the 21st Century*.

Craftspeople usually leave their work to speak for itself, so it is a rare privilege to have the thoughts, stories, experiences, observations and feelings of such skilled people in a book that enables us to share their insights on the nature of their work and the way they live.

Most have been featured in Resurgence magazine, which regularly features crafts and their connection with spirituality, ecology, and sustainable, joyful living.

The work of these creators comes from their great dedication to their craft and the sincerity with which they integrate their philosophy with daily life, in much the same way that their bowls and baskets, chairs and tables, shoes and spoons are art for daily use. Their words inspire, and their works delight. These essays, with beautiful accompanying colour photographs, encourage us to have faith in the human spirit and the human endeavour.

ISBN 978 1 903998 42 7   290 x 215mm
192pp in full colour, with over 120 photographs   £20.00 hb

IMAGES OF EARTH & SPIRIT
A Resurgence Art Anthology
Edited by John Lane and Satish Kumar

"Resurgence has been a longtime friend to artists looking to forge a meaningful relationship between art and soul. Readers who treasure this rich and varied artistic lineage may now enjoy its startlingly sensuous images within the pages of a single, elegantly designed book." — Suzi Gablik, author of *The Re-enchantment of Art* and *Living the Magical Life*.

Images of Earth & Spirit features the work of over fifty artists: over 140 sumptuous illustrations accompanied by interviews and insights into their work. Artists featured include Robin Baring, Cecil Collins, Alan Davie, Morris Graves, Andy Goldsworthy, Andrzej Jackowski, Richard Long, John Meirion Morris, David Nash, Margaret Neve, Peter Randall-Page, Haku Shah, Jane Siegle, Evelyn Williams and Christopher Wood.

All the artists have been featured in the pages of Resurgence magazine, an international forum for ecological and spiritual thinking. Besides challenging much of the conventional wisdom of our times (including the dream of unending material progress), Resurgence stresses the wisdom of beauty and, above all else, the holistic view — the relevance of interconnectedness. The work of these artists speaks of a new sense of the universe, a new sense of spirituality, holism and interconnectedness, openness and non-determinism. It gives hope for the renewal of life in the future.

ISBN 978 1 903998 29 8   290 x 215mm
192pp in full colour, with 147 illustrations   £20.00 hb

ONLY CONNECT
Soil, Soul, Society
The Best of Resurgence magazine 1990-1999
Edited by John Lane and Maya Kumar Mitchell

This outstanding selection of articles from Resurgence magazine commemorates the publication of the journal's 200th edition, and twenty-five years of the editorship of Satish Kumar and June Mitchell.

What is Resurgence? As the list of writers shows, it is a magazine of many ideas and insights which are helping to shape the coming age of ecology — an age which will bring together soil, soul and society. Among its themes are the fundamental destructiveness of the global economy; the need for 'economics as if people mattered'; the importance of human scale, spirituality, rurality, non-violence, and the Third World. Resurgence acknowledges the wisdom of beauty, the value of practical example and the importance of the whole, a holistic view of life. 'Only connect,' wrote E.M. Forster — it might preface every edition.

Contributors include Wendell Berry, Lester Brown, Fritjof Capra, Noam Chomsky, Herman Daly, Larry Dossey, Matthew Fox, Vaclav Havel, Paul Hawken, James Hillman, Ted Hughes, Wes Jackson, David Korten, James Lovelock, Wangari Maathai, Gita Mehta, Neil Postman, Kathleen Raine, Theodore Roszak, Vandana Shiva and Sting.

ISBN 978 1 870098 90 8   288pp   234 x 156mm   £12.95 pb